# THE
# SECULAR
# CREED

—

## ENGAGING FIVE
## CONTEMPORARY CLAIMS

Published by The Gospel Coalition

The Gospel Coalition
P.O. Box 170346
Austin, Texas 78717

Art Direction: Steven Morales
Cover Design: Gabriel Reyes-Ordeix
Typesetting: Ryan Leichty

ISBN:
978-0-9992843-0-8 (Print)
978-0-9992843-2-2 (Mobi)
978-0-9992843-1-5 (ePub)

*Printed in the United States of America*

"Addressing five key cultural topics of the day in this vital book, Rebecca McLaughlin deftly examines the pernicious lies that have insidiously infiltrated our world, including the church, and gives a solid and biblical rebuttal to each lie. Every Christian needs to read this book."

BECKET COOK, author of *A Change of Affection: A Gay Man's Incredible Story of Redemption* and host of "The Becket Cook Show"

"In this book, Rebecca McLaughlin offers a gentle, yet powerful biblical corrective that calls readers to holistic Christian love—a higher calling than the call of the culture, and, often, a harder calling. She examines popular cultural mantras and answers each one with the truth and application of the gospel of Christ. In her balanced and gracious approach, she paints our culture's arguments in the most compassionate light possible—and then shows the beauty of a more excellent way!"

JASMINE HOLMES, author of *Mother to Son: Letters to a Black Boy on Identity and Hope*

"Rebecca McLaughlin's first book was the best all-round defense of the Christian faith I had read in a decade. This one is the perfect complement. In it the author points the way to a different kind of 'muscular' Christianity, one that is able to flex the *muscle of conviction* and the *muscle of compassion* at the same time. For a church—and a world—too often forced to choose between smug conservatism and acquiescing liberalism, McLaughlin recovers the genius of Jesus Christ, showing us how to love the truth and humans with equal passion. The result is an utterly compelling and humane treatment of five vital contemporary issues."

JOHN DICKSON, author and historian, Distinguished Fellow in Public Christianity at Ridley College, Australia

"This book is so powerful on a thousand levels. It's compelling, accessible, informative, captivating, convicting, and empowering. It gives Christians understanding and language to be able to engage and not retreat, love and not compromise, accept and not affirm, empathize and not sympathize. It moves the conversation forward not just left or right. This is a discipleship book, not just an apologetics book. It's incredible."

CHRISTINE CAINE, founder, A21 & Propel Women

"There are few whose voices I trust more in translating the claims of Christ for a new generation than Rebecca McLaughlin. She writes with a gospel clarity, keenness of insight, and personal winsomeness that make her one of the best apologists of our generation. As with her debut book, *Confronting Christianity*, I enthusiastically endorse this one."

J. D. GREEAR, pastor, The Summit Church, Raleigh-Durham, North Carolina; president, Southern Baptist Convention

"Rebecca McLaughlin goes where few dare to go—head first into the hardest questions and issues of our cultural moment, with compassion, clarity, and conviction in order to show the beauty and cogency of the Christian faith. She is one of the most important writers serving the church today. She proved this with *Confronting Christianity* and has cemented that status with *The Secular Creed*. A potent blend of cultural analysis and biblical reflection, this is the rare book that's vital for believers and skeptics alike. I'm eager to get *The Secular Creed* into the hands of both my congregants and non-Christian friends."

CLAUDE ATCHO, pastor, Fellowship Memphis in Memphis, Tennessee; author of a forthcoming book on African American literature and theology (Brazos)

"The people around us care deeply about diversity, equality, and justice—and many think Christians stand against those values. As a pastor of a diverse, urban church, I need help to wisely and winsomely address their concerns. This is why I'm thankful for the major assist I've gotten from this book. McLaughlin knows today's issues well and has the biblical, historical, and sociological knowledge to help us understand them and be equipped to answer them well."

VERMON PIERRE, lead pastor, Roosevelt Community Church in Phoenix, Arizona; council member of The Gospel Coalition

# CONTENTS

*For Rachel,*
*and for everyone who longs for*
*justice, truth,*
*and love.*

# INTRODUCTION

"What does that mean?"

My 8-year-old held a bracelet she'd found at school. Stamped on its rim were three words: "Love Is Love." On our drive to church, we pass a hair salon, its windows filled with posters of George Floyd and massive, multicolored wings proclaiming, "Trans Lives Matter," "Black Lives Matter," "Love Is Love," "Better Together." Across our neighborhood, yard signs declare,

> In this house we believe that:
> Black Lives Matter
> Love Is Love
> Women's Rights Are Human Rights
> We Are All Immigrants
> Diversity Makes Us Stronger

Signs like this sketch out a secular creed or statement of belief. It centers not on God, but on diversity, equality, and everybody's right to be themselves.

Seeing signs like this, Christians tend to grab hammers. Some grab one to drive the sign into their lawn. They lament racial injustice, they believe in diversity, they know women are equal to men, and they've been taught that affirming gay relationships, trans identities, and pro-choice positions comes part and parcel with these other things. If black lives matter (which they surely do), then love of all kinds must be love. Others take up hammers with a different plan.

Knowing that the Bible rejects some things that underlie this modern creed, they swing a hammer to flatten the sign. Perhaps not literally, but in their hearts and minds. If these ideas stand together, they must all be wrong.

This book will offer a third approach. Wielding a marker instead of a mallet, it will consider five contemporary claims: "Black Lives Matter," "The Gay-Rights Movement Is the New Civil-Rights Movement," "Love Is Love," "Women's Rights Are Human Rights," and "Transgender Women Are Women." Examining each claim through the lens of Scripture and in light of culture, we'll aim to disentangle ideas Christians can and must affirm from ideas Christians cannot and must not embrace. But to wield the marker well, we must get down on our knees.

First, we must recognize that the tangling of ideas in the secular creed has been driven not only by sin in the world out there, but also by sin in the church in here. We must fall to our knees and repent. The frequent failure of Christians to meet biblical ideals of fellowship across racial difference, equal valuing of men and women, welcome for outcasts, love for those with unfulfilled desire, and care for the most marginalized has allowed this mixture of ideas to coalesce under the banner of diversity. But with our heads bowed to the earth, we'll see that the very ground in which the yard sign stands is unmistakably Christian. Clear that Christian soil away and you won't find solid, secular rock. You'll find a sinkhole.

To our 21st-century, Western ears, love across racial and cultural difference, the equality of men and women, and the idea that the poor, oppressed, and marginalized can make moral claims on the strong, rich, and powerful sound like basic moral common sense. But they are not. These truths have come to us from Christianity. Rip that foundation out, and you won't uncover a better basis for human equality and rights. You'll uncover an abyss that cannot even tell you what a human being is. Like cartoon characters running off a cliff, we may continue a short way before we realize that the ground has gone from underneath our feet. But it has gone. Without Christian beliefs about humanity, the yard sign's claims aren't worth the cardboard on which they are written.

So, when we pass these signs, I tell my children that in our house we believe that black lives matter because they matter to Jesus. We don't believe that love is love but that God is love, and that he gives us glimpses of his love through different kinds of relationship. We believe women's rights are human rights, because God made us—male and female—in his image; and for that same reason we believe that babies in the womb have rights as well. We believe God has a special concern for single mothers, orphans, and immigrants, because Scripture tells us so again and again. And we believe that diversity does indeed make us stronger, because Jesus calls people from every tribe and tongue and nation to worship him as one body together.

As you walk through this book, I hope you'll feel both humbled and empowered. If you're a follower of Jesus, I hope you'll be ready to join with the call to loving arms at the end. If you're not yet following Jesus, or if you couldn't imagine ever wanting to, I hope you'll see the moral soil on which you stand is more Christian than you realize. And I hope you'll start to wonder if the poor, first-century, brown-skinned, Jewish man known as Jesus of Nazareth—who lived as a member of an oppressed ethnic group and died at the hands of an imperial regime—might truly be the Savior of the world: the one who showed us what love is by laying down his life for us (1 John 3:16).

# 1

# "BLACK LIVES
# MATTER"

In Alabama in 1985, a black man named Anthony Ray Hinton was sentenced to death for double homicide. The conviction was based on a faulty ballistics report, but the prosecutor believed he could tell Hinton was guilty just by looking at him. Hinton's story is told in Bryan Stevenson's bestselling book, *Just Mercy* (2014).[1] In decades of representing poor clients on death row, Stevenson and his colleagues at the Equal Justice Initiative have won reversals, relief, or release for more than 115 condemned people. Many were convicted because white officers, lawyers, and jurors could tell they were guilty just by looking at them.

In June 2020, I watched the film based on Stevenson's book as Black Lives Matter protests multiplied. George Floyd had been slowly squeezed to death under the knee of a white police officer. Ahmaud Arbery had been hunted and shot to death by white vigilantes spitting racist slurs, and who had not initially been arrested for their crime. Breonna Taylor had been shot in her home by officers raiding the wrong house. Stevenson's book was already a bestseller. But the tales

1.   Bryan Stevenson, *Just Mercy: A Story of Justice and Redemption* (New York: Spiegel & Grau, 2014).

it told struck a new chord with me. Like many others, I was moved to tears as an elderly black man, whose mind had been wrecked by war, was executed, while his requested song, "The Old Rugged Cross," blared over the prison sound system. Story after story broke my heart. Person after person treated like their skin color made them criminals, like their lives didn't matter. What's more, these things had happened in my lifetime in a state recently ranked first in America for overall religiosity.[2]

As a white, Christian immigrant to America, learning about the history of race relations has disillusioned me. The bloody stain of racism that has been smeared across white churches for centuries continues to discolor Christian witness today. I understand why many of my friends see Black Lives Matter signs in part as anti-Christian protest. But while *Just Mercy* tells harrowing tales of black oppression, it also gives us glimpses of black faith: not least the faith of Stevenson himself, whose own deep-seated hope in Christ has driven his pursuit of justice.[3] In the closing minutes of the film, we see footage of the real Hinton walking free after 30 years on death row, and we hear his sister, embracing him with tears of joy, sob out the film's last words: "Thank you, Jesus! Thank you, Lord!"

The question at the heart of this chapter is how Christians should relate to the statement "Black lives matter." We all bring different sensitivities. For many black Christians, it feels like an utterly self-evident truth: a claim they are tired of having to make, three words to voice centuries of anger, fear, and pain. For some white Christians, it feels like a rallying cry: a way to protest the racial injustice of which they have been keenly aware. For others, it sounds like an attack: an accusation of racism that feels unwarranted and unfair. And for still

2. According to a 2016 survey, 51 percent of people in Alabama attend church at least weekly and 82 percent believe in God with certainty, https://www.pewresearch.org/fact-tank/2016/02/29/how-religious-is-your-state/?state=alabama.

3. Stevenson talks about his faith in Dominique Dubois Gilliard, "Bryan Stevenson Wants to Liberate People from the Lie That Their Life Doesn't Matter," *Christianity Today*, January 10, 2020, https://www.christianitytoday.com/ct/2020/january-web-only/just-mercy-film-bryan-stevenson.html. See also this dialogue with Tim Keller: "Grace, Justice and Mercy: An Evening with Bryan Stevenson & Rev. Tim Keller Q&A," https://www.youtube.com/watch?v=32CHZiVFmB4.

others, it feels like the spearhead of a progressive agenda: a wolf in sheep's clothing that must be exposed.

In this chapter, we'll dig under the topsoil of the black lives matter claim. We'll see that, far from being the enemy of love across racial difference, Christianity is its first and enduring foundation. We'll see that God created humans of all racial backgrounds equal, and that God's covenant people included black and brown folk from the first. We'll see that Jesus broke through every racial and cultural barrier of his day and commanded his disciples to make disciples of all nations. We'll meet the first African believers, who were following Jesus centuries before the gospel came to America, and we'll see that today Christianity is the most racially, culturally, and geographically diverse belief system in the world. Finally, we'll see that the reason we believe in love across racial difference now is because of Jesus—whether we realize it or not.

## IN THE BEGINNING

In 1776, the Declaration of Independence proclaimed, "We hold these truths to be self-evident, that all men are created equal." But human equality is not self-evident at all. Israeli historian Yuval Noah Harari explains:

> The Americans got the idea of equality from Christianity, which argues that every person has a divinely created soul, and that all souls are equal before God. However, if we do not believe in the Christian myths about God, creation and souls, what does it mean that all people are "equal"?[4]

The first chapter of the Bible claims that God made human beings *in his image* (Gen. 1:26). If this is not true, then there is no basis for equality and rights. Writing as an atheist, Harari explains that "*Homo Sapiens* has no natural rights, just as spiders, hyenas, and chimpanzees have no natural rights."[5]

4.   Yuval Noah Harari, *Sapiens: A Brief History of Humankind* (New York: Harper, 2015), 109.
5.   Harari, *Sapiens*, 111.

We must not be naïve about the past. The painful reality is that the founding fathers excluded enslaved Africans from their vision of human equality. But this problem isn't fixed by erasing the basis for equality. In fact, the dehumanizing ways in which black people were treated by white slaveholders were only truly *wrong* if human beings are truly more than animals, if love across racial difference is *right*, and if *right* and *wrong* are universal. The rational atheist can cling to none of these things.

If the Bible is true, however, God didn't just make our souls. He made our bodies. He made black people and white people, Asian people and Latino people, people from every tribe and tongue and nation, all equally *in his image*. This is the soil in which the roots of human equality grow. But the Bible doesn't stop there. It tells a story that begins with humans from all sorts of ethnicities becoming God's people, and that ends with people from every tribe and tongue and nation worshiping Jesus together.

## MIXED MULTITUDE

In Genesis 12, God called a man from a city located in modern-day Iraq. God promised to make this man, Abraham, a great nation and that in him "all the families of the earth" would be blessed (Gen. 12:2–3). This promise is ultimately fulfilled in Christ: the descendant of Abraham who would open the floodgates of God's blessing to engulf people from every nation on earth. But even from the first, God wove different ethnicities into his covenant people.

Abraham's grandson Jacob had 12 sons who became the 12 tribes of Israel. But one son, Joseph, was sold by his brothers and became a slave in Egypt. Joseph helped Egypt survive a famine, saved his family, and married an Egyptian woman, Asenath (Gen. 41:45). Together, they had Ephraim and Manasseh. Jacob blessed these boys and prophesied that they would grow into a multitude (Gen. 48). As New Testament scholar Esau McCaulley puts it, "African blood flows *into* Israel from the beginning as a fulfilment of the promise made to Abraham, Isaac and Jacob."[6]

During 400 years in Egypt, the Israelites went from being honored immigrants to being slaves. God sent Moses to rescue them. Moses had married Zipporah, a woman from Midian (in modern-day Saudi Arabia), and had children with her. When he led the Israelites out of Egypt, a "mixed multitude" left with them—likely including Egyptians who had seen God act and decided to join his people (Ex. 12:38). After the exodus (perhaps after Zipporah's death), Moses married a Cushite woman: in today's terms, an Ethiopian (Num. 12:1). Centuries of Western art have pictured God's covenant people as white. But the Israelites who wandered in the wilderness were from the Middle East and Africa. As the story of God's people unfolds, we see even more ethnicities woven in.

## JESUS'S DNA

Thanks to a document passed down in my husband's family, we know that one of his ancestors was Cherokee. Her name was Eliza, and our second daughter is named after her. In modern, Western culture, few of us bother to trace our lineage back more than a few generations. But when Jesus was born, genealogies were highly prized.

Matthew's genealogy of Jesus particularly highlights the non-Israelite women in his ancestry, such as Rahab, the Canaanite prostitute who believed the Israelites' God was truly "God in the heavens above and on the earth beneath" (Josh. 2:12; Matt. 1:5), and Ruth the Moabite, whose story generated a whole Old Testament book. In Matthew's retelling of Israel's history, we see that non-Israelites weren't just squeezed in at the fringes of God's purposes. They were plumbed into the royal bloodline.

Jesus's DNA was shaped by Rahab and by Ruth. He had non-Israelite blood in his veins. And when he preached, it showed.

---

6.   Esau McCaulley, *Reading While Black: African American Biblical Interpretation as an Exercise in Hope* (Downers Grove, IL: IVP Academic, 2020), 102.

## SCANDAL OF JESUS'S FIRST SERMON

Jesus's first sermon in his hometown lit a fire of justice that's been burning ever since. He began by reading from the prophet Isaiah:

> The Spirit of the Lord is upon me,
>     because he has anointed me
>     to proclaim good news to the poor.
> He has sent me to proclaim liberty to the captives
>     and recovering of sight to the blind,
>     to set at liberty those who are oppressed,
>     to proclaim the year of the Lord's favor. (Luke 4:18–19)

Jesus claimed to have fulfilled these words. They represent one New Testament text among many that hammer justice for the poor, oppressed, and wrongly imprisoned into the heart of God's concern for his world. At first, the response from Jesus's Jewish audience was good. Living under Roman oppression, they longed for a Messiah who would set them free and establish them politically. Maybe Jesus was their long-awaited champion! But they also wanted proof that Jesus was as good as his promise. After all, they'd watched him grow up.

Instead of performing a miracle or celebrating Jewish history, however, Jesus started showcasing how God has always cared for Gentiles (Luke 4:25–27). Jesus's fellow countrymen were so furious they tried to kill him (Luke 4:28–30). His multiethnic message was the last thing they wanted to hear. But this didn't put Jesus off. Quite the reverse.

## SCANDAL OF THE GOOD SAMARITAN

At age 18, I spent a summer working in Manhattan. One hot evening, I was going for dinner at a friend's apartment, and I bought a watermelon for dessert. When my friend opened the door, she looked uncomfortable. She told me she'd never eaten a watermelon. "Why not?" I asked, "They're delicious!" My friend graciously explained to me the long history of people associating African Americans with watermelon. As a black woman, she'd always avoided the fruit. I'd grown up in England. I had no idea.

When we step into the pages of the Scriptures, we're all immigrants. There are things we won't instinctively grasp, not least about ethnicity. We hear "Samaritan" and think, *Good!* But for Jews of Jesus's day, Samaritans were both racially and religiously despised. We don't feel the shock of Jesus's famous story of the Good Samaritan. But his first audience did.

A lawyer asked Jesus, "What shall I do to inherit eternal life?" Jesus asked a question in return: "What is written in the law?" The lawyer responded, "You shall love the Lord your God with all your heart and with all your soul and with all your strength and with all your mind, and your neighbor as yourself." Jesus agreed. But then the lawyer asked, "Who is my neighbor?" Jesus responded with a story in which a man, likely Jewish, is robbed and assaulted and left for dead on his way from Jerusalem to Jericho. Two Jewish religious leaders walk by before a Samaritan rescues the man. Jesus asked the lawyer which of the men who came by was a neighbor to the assault victim. The lawyer, who couldn't bring himself to say "the Samaritan," replied, "The one who showed him mercy" (Luke 10:25–37).

When we read this story, we hear a call to care for strangers in need. But Jesus's first audience heard more. They heard a story of love across racial, religious, and political difference, in which the moral hero was their sworn enemy. This story isn't just a call to love. It's a call to love across racial, cultural, and ideological barriers built up over generations. It's a call to love those we were raised to hate. It's a call that should have made segregation in America and apartheid in South Africa impossible.

Luke doesn't tell us how the crowd reacted to Jesus's story. But if we map the racial and political divides of his day onto ours, perhaps we can imagine what might've been said. "It's all very well Jesus telling this idealistic story about a *good* Samaritan, but what about all the *bad* Samaritans? Have you heard about the crime rates in Samaria? And all the teenage pregnancies? I'd have no problem with Samaritans if they really *were* good."

If we're honest, we all have groups we like to dismiss. Lifelong Republicans know Democrats are immoral. Dyed-in-the-wool Democrats know the same about Republicans. The white prosecutor could tell that Hinton was guilty just by looking at him. Jews could tell the same about Samaritans. When my non-Christian friends hear about another celebrity pastor caught in a sex scandal, they're not surprised: they know Christians are hypocrites. When we hear about violence against someone from a group we suspect, we look for evidence that they deserved it. When we see violence from a group we trust, we look for evidence that it was justified. But Jesus devastates our them-and-us mentality, not just through a story about a good Samaritan, but also through a stunning conversation with a bad one.

## SCANDAL OF THE BAD SAMARITAN

In John 4, Jesus sat down by a well, while his disciples went to buy food. A Samaritan woman came to draw water. Jesus asked her for a drink. There are two problems with this. First, the woman is a Samaritan, and Jews had no dealings with Samaritans. Second, a respectable Jewish rabbi shouldn't be talking alone with a woman. She's shocked. "How is that you, a Jew, ask for a drink from me, a woman of Samaria?" But as the story unfolds, we find out there's another problem. This woman has had five husbands and is now living with a man she's not married to. By the Jewish standards of the day, she's about as bad as a woman could be. But what do you expect? She's a Samaritan, after all. Jesus should've known she was guilty just by looking at her. But as their conversation progresses, we discover that he did (John 4:4–26).

Jesus's discussion with this sinful woman from a hated racial and religious group is the longest private conversation he had with *anyone* in the Gospels. She's also the first person in John's Gospel to whom Jesus reveals his identity as the Messiah. When Jesus's disciples return, she goes back to her town and tells her fellow Samaritans about him. Many believe in Jesus because of her testimony (John 4:39). Jesus knew precisely what he was doing when he asked this woman for a drink. He was recruiting the last person even the Samaritans would've listened to and trusting her to be his messenger. Just as he made the fictional Good Samaritan into a moral hero, so he makes this real, live Bad Samaritan into a missionary.

Jesus tears down the racial and cultural barriers of his day and dances on the rubble.

## MAKE DISCIPLES OF ALL NATIONS

Jesus's public ministry was mostly focused on his fellow Jews. But time and again, he commends the faith of those outside the Jewish fold. He praises the faith of a Roman centurion (Matt. 8:5–13) and a Syrophoenician woman (Matt. 15:21–28). When he heals 10 lepers, the only one who turns back to thank him is a Samaritan, whose faith Jesus commends (Luke 17:11–19). And after his resurrection, Jesus declares, "All authority in heaven and on earth has been given to me" and tells his followers, "Go therefore and make disciples of all nations" (Matt. 28:18–19).

Jesus was the one through whom all things were made (John 1:3). He created every ethnicity, and he calls people from every tribe and tongue and nation to himself. Centuries of colonialism have left many people thinking that the first black Christians emerged when European missionaries went to Africa. But if we read the Bible, we find the first black people coming to Christ on Day One of the church.

## FIRST BLACK CHRISTIANS

When the Spirit is poured out at Pentecost, the apostles preach to people "from every nation under heaven," including those from modern-day Iran, Iraq, Turkey, Egypt, and Libya (Acts 2:5–11). Three thousand came to Christ. This is the birthday of the church. On this day, Middle Easterners, Africans, and Europeans started worshiping Jesus together. Luke tells us what this looked like. These first Christians devoted themselves to the apostles' teaching, to fellowship, to breaking of bread, and to prayer. They were selling their possessions and sharing their money with any who had need. They were worshiping together and eating together in each other's homes (Acts 2:42–47). This wasn't just gathering at the same church on Sunday. This was life together. But the Bible doesn't just scan the multiethnic crowd. It also zooms in on individuals.

In Acts 8, an angel of the Lord sends Philip to a highly educated Ethiopian man, who is sitting in his chariot reading from Isaiah 53. This passage subverts every modern stereotype. In the framework that tried to justify slavery and segregation in America, black people were repeatedly painted as morally, spiritually, and intellectually inferior. But this account of the first known black Christian skewers those ideas. In a world in which few were literate, this man is reading God's Word when Philip finds him. As humble as he is learned, the Ethiopian welcomes Philip eagerly. Beginning with the description of the suffering servant in Isaiah 53, Philip tells him "the good news about Jesus" (Acts 8:35). As soon as they find water this man asks to be baptized (Acts 8:36). His enthusiasm leaps from the page.

Luke includes three details about the Ethiopian, in addition to his ethnicity. First, Luke tells us he was a eunuch. Second, that he was a court official of Candice, queen of the Ethiopians, responsible for all her treasure. Third, that he had come to Jerusalem to worship (Acts 8:27). This man was both honored and marginalized. He had a position of great authority and trust. But he was also a eunuch who had been castrated as a child and was likely technically a slave. He was already a worshiper of God, but he hadn't yet met Jesus. If we read Isaiah 53 in context, we find it is the perfect entry point for this man. We see God's suffering servant, pierced for our transgressions, despised and rejected by men, achieving victory through pain. And as Isaiah's prophecy continues, we see specific promises to foreigners and eunuchs who trust in the Lord.[7]

In Acts 8, we don't just see an individual black Christian, whose life mattered to God so much that his angel sent an apostle to help with his Bible study. We also see the continuity between the Old Testament and the New, as God's promises to foreigners who trust him are fleshed out. We see hope for those whose bodies have been violated and for those unable to have children. And we see a black man

---

7.    "Let not the foreigner who has joined himself to the Lord say, 'The Lord will surely separate me from his people'; and let the eunuch not say, 'Behold I am a dry tree.' For thus says the Lord: 'To the eunuchs who keep my Sabbaths, who choose the things that please me and hold fast to my covenant, I will give in my house and within my walls a monument and a name better than sons and daughters; I will give them an everlasting name that shall not be cut off'" (Isa. 56:3–5).

going on his way rejoicing because he had new life in Jesus Christ (Acts 8:39).

## MULTIETHNIC HEARTBEAT OF THE NEW TESTAMENT

As the story of the newborn church unfolds, we hear its multiethnic heartbeat. The church blossoms from its Jewish roots to include more and more Gentiles. The followers of Jesus were first called Christians in Antioch, the ruins of which lie in Turkey (Acts 11:26). Because we're all immigrants to the text, it's harder for us to see the racial and ethnic walls being demolished by the gospel wrecking ball. But that's what is happening. Paul wrote to the first Christians in Turkey, "Here there is not Greek and Jew, circumcised and uncircumcised, barbarian, Scythian, slave, free; but Christ is all, and in all" (Col. 3:11).

The Jew-Gentile divide was deeply ingrained in Jewish consciousness, and Paul speaks to it in two ways: Jew versus Greek, and circumcised versus uncircumcised. He also knocks down the slave-free divide in a culture that assumed slavery was normal and in which at least one person in three would've been enslaved. Unlike slavery in America, first-century slavery was largely not race-based, so this was not a comment on ethnicity. But Paul also speaks to racial and cultural divides when he mentions barbarians and Scythians. These terms mean almost nothing to us. We don't turn on the news and hear about barbarian immigrants or Scythian refugees. But writing to America today, Paul might have said of the church: "Here there is no black American or white American, Asian American or Latino American, there is no rich or poor, no immigrant or native born, but Christ is all, and in all." Love across racial difference isn't just a modern, progressive ideal. It started as a biblical ideal. Interracial love is part of our inheritance in Christ.

When we refuse fellowship across racial and cultural difference, we're tearing Jesus's beautiful body apart.

## GREAT MULTITUDE NO ONE COULD NUMBER

In the biblical finale, John witnesses the greatest multiracial, multiethnic, multicultural gathering ever seen:

> After this I looked, and behold, a great multitude that no one could
> number, from every nation, from all tribes and peoples and languag-
> es, standing before the throne and before the Lamb, clothed in white
> robes, with palm branches in their hands and crying out with a loud
> voice, "Salvation belongs to our God, who sits on the throne and to the
> Lamb!" (Rev. 7:9–10)

At Pentecost, the Spirit inspired the apostles to speak in different
languages, so all heard the message in their native tongue. Christianity
is not only multiethnic. It's also multicultural, and we should expect
Christians to speak different languages, sing different songs, eat different foods, wear different clothes, and bring different insights to God's
universal, timeless Word. At the same time, we must pursue love and
fellowship across racial and cultural difference relentlessly—not because progressives tell us to, but because Jesus calls us to be one body
with people of different races and cultures and languages. Worshiping
Jesus together is our destiny. But it is also becoming our reality.

Today, Christianity is the largest and the most diverse belief system in the world, with roughly equal numbers of Christians in Europe, North America, South America, and Africa,[8] and with a rapidly
growing church in China that is expected to outgrow the church in
America by 2030, and could include half of China's population by
2060.[9] By that point, 40 percent of the world's Christians could be
living in sub-Saharan Africa. If the experts are right, I will likely live
to see black Christians become the largest racial group within the
global church.

White progressives who dismiss Christianity because they associate it with white racism are failing to listen to black believers globally.

---

8.   See "The Future of World Religions: Population Growth Projections, 2010–2050," Pew Re-
     search Center, April 2, 2015, http://www.pewforum.org/2015/04/02/religious-projections-2010-
     2050, and "Projected Change in Global Population, 2015–2060," Pew Research Center, March
     31, 2017, http://www.pewforum.org/2017/04/05/the-changing-global-religiouslandscape/
     pf_17-04-05_projectionsupdate_changepopulation640px.
9.   See Pew Research Center Global Religious Survey, 2010, cited by Eleanor Albert, "Chris-
     tianity in China," Council on Foreign Relations, March 9, 2018, https://www.cfr.org/back-
     grounder/christianity-china. See also "Prison Sentence for Pastor Shows China Feels Threat-
     ened by Spread of Christianity, Experts Say," TIME, January 2, 2020, https://time.com/5757591/
     wang-yi-prison-sentence-china-christianity.

They're also failing to listen to black people in America, who are almost 10 percentage points more likely than their white peers to identify as Christians, and who poll higher on every measure of Christian commitment, from churchgoing to Bible-reading to core evangelical beliefs.[10] Both globally and in the United States, black women are the most typical Christians. As Yale Law professor Stephen L. Carter writes, "When you mock Christians, you're not mocking who you think you are."[11]

These facts don't for a moment excuse the history of white Christians treating black people as if their lives didn't matter. We'll examine that problem more fully in chapter 3. But dismissing Christianity because of the failure of white Christians means silencing the voices of black believers and acting like only white voices matter in considering Christ.

## LISTENING TO BLACK VOICES

In *Reading While Black: African American Biblical Interpretation as an Exercise in Hope*, New Testament professor and *New York Times* contributing author Esau McCaulley invites us to listen to the full choir of African American Christians. Theologically liberal black authors, who emphasize justice here-and-now at the expense of what the Bible teaches about eternal justice, are often seen by secular progressives and by white evangelicals as primary voices of black faith. This is convenient for both sides: it allows secular progressives to dismiss full-blooded Christianity, and all too often it allows white evangelicals to dismiss the critiques of black believers. But in reality, most black churches in America are theologically evangelical, even if that increasingly politicized word isn't a comfortable fit. For example, 85 percent of members of historically black churches see the Bible as the Word

---

10.   See, for example, David Masci, "5 Facts about the Religious Lives of African Americans," Pew Research Center, February 7, 2018, http://www.pewresearch.org/facttank/2018/02/07/5-facts-about-the-religious-lives-of-african-americans.

11.   Stephen L. Carter, "The Ugly Coded Critique of Chick-fil-A's Christianity," Bloomberg, April 21, 2018, https://www.bloomberg.com/opinion/articles/2018-04-21/criticism-of-christians-and-chick-fil-a-has-troubling-roots.

of God, versus only 62 percent of mainline Christians.[12] Meanwhile, 82 percent of Christians at historically black churches believe in the reality of hell: the same percentage as among self-identifying evangelicals.[13] To listen to black voices, people on all sides must reckon with the gospel-centered, Bible-believing stance of most black churches.

Listening will be as uncomfortable for the white Christian conservative as for the secular progressive. A Bible-believing Christian himself, McCaulley explains,

> It is difficult for the African American believer to look deeply into the history of Christianity and not be profoundly shaken. Insomuch as it arises in response to the church's historic mistreatment of African Americans, the Black secular protest against religion is one of the most understandable developments in the history of the West. If they are wrong (and they are) it is a wrongness born out of considerable pain.[14]

As a white evangelical, I could easily gloss over this pain. The chronic sin of white Christian racism dishonors the name of Christ. The slow-burn holocaust of black lives across the centuries is hard to face. To pause here is uncomfortable. But Jesus doesn't call us to be comfortable. He calls us to repentance and faith. And when we pause, we'll realize that the loudest voices of protest *against* white Christian racism have been from fellow Christians. While many white Christians were complicit in race-based slavery, McCaulley reminds us that "the widespread move to abolish slavery [was] a Christian innovation,"[15] that "Black conversion to Christ began on a large scale during the Great Awakening of the mid-eighteenth century,"[16] and that "early

12.   See Jeff Diamant, "Blacks more likely than others in U.S. to read the Bible regularly, see it as God's word," Pew Research Center, December 16, 2020, https://www.pewresearch.org/fact-tank/2018/05/07/blacks-more-likely-than-others-in-u-s-to-read-the-bible-regularly-see-it-as-gods-word, based on 2014 Pew Forum survey data.

13.   See Caryle Murphy, "Most Americans believe in heaven . . . and hell," Pew Research Center, November 10, 2015, https://www.pewresearch.org/fact-tank/2015/11/10/most-americans-be-lieve-in-heaven-and-hell.

14.   McCaulley, *Reading While Black*, 135.

15.   McCaulley, *Reading While Black*, 142.

16.   McCaulley, *Reading While Black*, 169.

Black Christians combined a strong affirmation of the need for personal salvation with varying levels of social action and resistance."[17]

Civil-rights heroes like Fannie Lou Hamer and the Reverend Doctor Martin Luther King Jr. are rightly celebrated by secular people. But their message was unrelentingly Christian. Like Old Testament prophets, they called out the sin of those who claimed to know the Lord but were not living in his ways. They called for Americans to be *more* Christian, not less. Today, the most celebrated black leaders are often progressives. But they don't represent most black Americans, who are neither secular nor theologically liberal.

Amid the 2020 Black Lives Matter protests, I went for a walk with a friend who directs the children's ministry at a multiethnic church. She told me that in the previous few months, she'd received messages from multiple friends and acquaintances—including people she hadn't seen since middle school—asking how she was and what they could do. She joked that she seemed to be lots of people's one black friend. But her response to each well-wisher was the same: "I'd love to talk to you about Jesus." One friend responded, "Do you really think that's the answer?" She replied that she did. And she is right, but not in the sense that Christians sometimes think.

At times, Christians have tried to close down conversations about racial justice by urging people to "Just preach the gospel." They suggest that pursuing racial justice is a distraction from the church's central mission of evangelism, and that if we preach the gospel of Jesus's death in our place, and the need for personal salvation, all other ills will naturally be healed. But Jesus didn't tell his disciples to just preach the gospel. He told them to "make disciples of all nations, baptizing them in the name of the Father and of the Son and of the Holy Spirit, teaching them to observe all that I have commanded you" (Matt. 28:19–20). As a Christian, I believe I'm saved by Jesus's death in my place, paying the price for my sin, and bringing me back into fellowship with God. Nothing can add to or take away from this. But because I've placed my trust in Christ, he is my King, and I must walk in his ways. Living as a disciple of Jesus includes preaching the gospel (Matt. 28:19), pursuing justice for the poor, oppressed and margin-

17.  McCaulley, *Reading While Black*, 175.

alized (Matt. 25:31–46), and practicing love across racial and cultural difference (Luke 10:25–37).

## SECULAR SINKHOLE

For most Westerners today, the alternative to Christianity isn't another religion. For all the contemporary interest in meditation, yoga, and what we see as ancient Eastern wisdom, few are looking for a full embrace of Buddhist or Hindu ethics. Radical Islam's association with violence and oppression of women tends not to appeal. And while Jewish religious and cultural practices are deeply precious even to avowedly atheist Jews, few curious gentiles find themselves in shul. For a growing proportion of people in the West, not identifying with any particular religion but retaining beliefs about human equality has felt like a safe place to land. After all, people reason, religion has done more harm than good and things like universal human rights, racial justice, and care for the poor are self-evident truths.

But as we saw at the beginning of this chapter, if there is no God who created us in his image, then human equality is a myth. Human beings have "no natural rights, just as spiders, hyenas, and chimpanzees have no natural rights."[18] Science cannot save this situation. As Yuval Noah Harari points out, "belief in the unique worth and rights of human beings . . . has embarrassingly little in common with the scientific study of *Homo sapiens*."[19] In fact, if we look to evolution as our *only* origin story and try to squeeze our ethics from its scientific husk, we have (at best) the idea that one should sacrifice only for members of one's genetic group. The idea of loving those whose origins lie in a different continent is dead in the primeval water. In fact, as atheist psychologist Steven Pinker observes, if virtue is equated with "sacrifices that benefit one's own group in competition with other groups . . . then fascism [is] the ultimate virtuous ideology."[20]

18. Harari, *Sapiens*, 111
19. Harari, *Sapiens*, 253.
20. Steven Pinker, "The False Allure of Group Selection," Edge, June 18, 2012, https://www.edge.org/conversation/steven_pinker-the-false-allureof-group-selection.

None of these points suggests that secular people don't believe in love across racial difference. Many do. But they do so on the basis of unanchored faith, clinging (whether they realize it or not) to a raft of Christian beliefs. In 2019, Notre Dame professor Christian Smith published *Atheist Overreach: What Atheism Can't Deliver*, in which he examined whether today's leading atheist intellectuals provide convincing reasons for their high moral beliefs. His conclusion? They do not. An atheist can believe in human rights if she likes. She can campaign for racial justice, volunteer at a soup kitchen, support NGOs that combat famine, and give to charities opposing sex trafficking. But she has no rational grounds for saying that *everyone* should believe in human rights, or that racism is unquestionably *wrong*. In a world without God, I may hate race-based slavery in the same sense that I hate olives. But at the end of the day, it comes down to personal preference.[21] So why do so many people today who identify as atheists, agnostics, or "nones" believe in universal human rights?

Historian Tom Holland explains that our basic moral beliefs about human equality came to us from Christianity, but that they have been deliberately rebranded as secular. In the late 1940s, with the world reeling from the horrors of the Second World War, Eleanor Roosevelt gathered representatives from various nations to establish a universal declaration of rights that would work in different cultures, including those in which Christianity was not dominant. So, Christian thinking had to be repackaged in non-religious terms. "A doctrine such as that of human rights," Holland observes, "was far likelier to be signed up for" if its Christian origins could be concealed.[22]

This rebranding has worked so well that even atheists now hold some Christian beliefs to be self-evident truths. The belief that every human life is valuable, that the oppressed and marginalized deserve justice, that we should love those whose race or culture or country is different from ours, that we should even love our enemies—these beliefs all come to us from a first-century Jewish rabbi who died on

21. For a version of this argument, see Christian Smith, *Atheist Overreach: What Atheism Can't Deliver* (New York: Oxford University Press, 2019), 49. As Tim Keller puts it, "While there can be moral *feelings* without God, it doesn't appear that there can be moral *obligation*." Timothy Keller, *Making Sense of God: An Invitation to the Skeptical* (New York: Viking, 2016), 173.

22. Holland, *Dominion*, 521.

a cross and whose resurrection spawned the greatest movement for diversity in history. Without Christianity, belief in human rights, in racial equality, and in the responsibility of the powerful toward the victimized becomes blind faith. The claim that black lives matter is at heart a Christian claim.

## 'IS THIS A JESUS SONG?'

My daughters attend a public school that celebrates diversity. But sometimes, when they come home with a new song, I point out that what they have learned was originally a Jesus song: "Amazing Grace" sung in Navajo, without explanation of the words. "I've Got Peace Like a River" and "We Shall Overcome" taught without reference to their gospel origins. Now, my girls will ask me, "Mummy, is this a Jesus song?"

Some white Christians worry that saying the specific words "Black lives matter" signals a wholesale embrace of progressive views. This is an understandable concern. As we will see in the next chapter, the Black Lives Matter organization presents racial justice as a package deal with celebrating LGBT+ romance and identity. We must carefully disentangle these differences. Still, many theological conservatives— including many black Christians—are glad to march under the "Black Lives Matter" sign because these words are a statement of truth.

Given the history of white evangelical failure to recognize black people as their equals before God, I gladly affirm that black lives matter, despite the fact an organization with that name expresses other beliefs I cannot embrace. If there were a secular organization called Unborn Babies Matter, I would say those words, too, even if that organization also waved a rainbow flag, because unborn babies matter. If I were concerned people might think I affirmed everything else that organization stood for, I'd simply add two words: "Unborn babies matter *to Jesus*."

Some respond that *all* lives matter. But this qualifier misses the point. For centuries, black people have been treated like their lives *didn't* matter. That's the problem being addressed, the truth that needs to be upheld, just as we'd recognize that "unborn babies matter" needs to be said. But we must also recognize that from a consistently atheistic perspective, *no* lives ultimately matter. Human beings have no natural rights, just as spiders, chimpanzees, and hyenas have no natural rights. Ultimately, black lives matter not because progressive people have told us so, but because the equal value of every human, regardless of race, walks off the pages of Scripture with the sound of a trumpet. Black lives matter enough for the Son of God to shed his blood, so that black men and women might have eternal life with him. Black lives matter because Jesus says so.

Christians must work for justice for historically crushed and marginalized people, because Jesus came to bring good news to the poor and to set at liberty those who are oppressed. Christians should be the first to fight for racial justice and to pursue love across racial difference, not because of any cultural pressure from outside, but because of scriptural pressure from inside. "Black lives matter" is at heart a Jesus song, and we must sing our Savior's songs, no matter who else plays the tune.

As we hear the tear-stained words of Anthony Ray Hinton's sister—"Thank you, Jesus! Thank you, Lord!"—we must ask: Why would a black woman in a state with one of the worst records on racial justice and one of the highest levels of Christian identification thank Jesus for her innocent brother's release? Because she knows that Jesus is on the side of the poor, oppressed, and falsely accused. Because she knows that black people have been followers of Jesus from the first. Because she knows that black lives like her brother's matter, not because a progressive organization bearing that name has capitalized on a cultural moment, but because black lives matter to Jesus.

# 2

# "LOVE IS LOVE"

"How do you know that what you say tomorrow will be safe?"

I was sitting in a small-town coffee shop in Missouri. A local church had invited me to speak on gender and sexuality, and local LGBT+ leaders had organized a protest. One leader had tweeted to warn others about the event and said I wasn't qualified to speak about such topics. I replied that she was probably right and asked if she'd be willing to meet for coffee while I was in town, so I could learn from her. She kindly consented and asked if she could bring her partner. I said I'd love to meet her. As we talked, I learned that these women had met at a church youth group and were now raising two daughters. Given the high suicide rates among LGBT+ youth, they were concerned that what I would say might not be safe for vulnerable young people.

When the question came, I'd heard how the sexual sin of leaders in their church had hurt and disillusioned them, and how they'd found joy and safety in each other. I liked these women. I felt I understood the choices they'd made. With their experiences, perhaps I would've done the same. When I shared my story of having been romantically attracted to women since childhood, but of choosing not to pursue those attractions and ultimately to marry a man, I hoped it would build trust. But they said my story was harmful. I hadn't seen that coming, and I was trying not to cry. When one woman asked, "How do you know that what you say tomorrow will be safe?" I had nothing left. "I don't," I replied. "Jesus said that if anyone wants to come after him, they must deny themselves and take up their cross and follow him. It isn't safe."

In this chapter, we'll turn our attention to the mantra "Love is love." We'll explore why, attractive as it sounds, it isn't ultimately true: we all need different *kinds* of love, and sexual and romantic intimacy is only one spoke in the wheel that makes the world go around. I'll argue instead that "God is love" (1 John 4:8) and that he shows us what that statement means through different kinds of human relationships. This makes Christianity good news for same-sex-attracted people like me. But it doesn't make Christianity safe. Whatever our attractions, following Jesus means denying ourselves and taking up our cross. But if Jesus's people are truly living in his ways, there's room and joy and love enough for all.

## IN THE BEGINNING

In chapter 1, we unearthed the cornerstone of human equality in the first chapter of the Bible. God's first words on sexuality are etched on that same stone. In Genesis 1, God creates humans—male and fe-male—*in his image*, and tells them to "be fruitful and multiply" (Gen. 1:28). If you think about it, God could've made humans some other way. We could've reproduced asexually, like amoebas—or like the python in the St. Louis Zoo that in July 2020 laid seven eggs without a mate. Instead, God designed us so that new humans come to be when men and women come together. This is the original diversity. Creation of new life comes through love across this difference.

In Genesis 2, we zoom in on a particular relationship between a paradigmatic man and woman. After calling his creation "good" and "very good" (Gen. 1:31), God says that it's "not good" for the man to be alone (Gen. 2:18). He makes woman as man's match and equal: *bone of his bone* and *flesh of his flesh* (Gen. 1:23). And then we read these enig-matic words: "Therefore a man shall leave his father and his mother and hold fast to his wife, and they shall become one flesh" (Gen. 2:24). Too often in church, we've acted like this is the end of the biblical story on sexuality. But it's only the beginning.

As we read on, we find that marriage isn't the goal of human existence. It's not the mountaintop. It's not the destination. It's a signpost.

## YOUR MAKER IS YOUR HUSBAND

In the age before smartphones, you needed a camera to snap photos. When the little roll of film was full, you took it to be developed. Days later, you'd pick up your prints, and in a pocket at the front of the packet, you'd find negatives: small squares of black and white that, when held up to the light, revealed the outlines of your images. Too often, when Christians look at what the Bible has to say about sexuality, we only see the negatives. We see the sexual boundaries we can't cross, and we clutch the little monochrome of human marriage to our hearts as if it were the ultimate thing. We miss that in the Bible this tiny negative is developed into a stunning, wall-sized print. To see that bigger, brighter, much more beautiful vision, we must soak in a river that starts in Genesis, swells through the prophets, bursts its banks in the Gospels, and becomes a mighty flood in Revelation: the river of God's passionate love for us.

The Ethiopian eunuch we met in chapter 1 was reading from Isaiah 53 when Philip ran up to his chariot. If they had read further down the scroll, they would have reached a shocking metaphor: God's rocky, cosmic marriage to his people. Isaiah 54 begins with a "barren one" being called on to sing, because "the children of the desolate one will be more than the children of her who is married" (Isa. 54:1). The language builds and builds until we realize that God isn't talking only about women who are childless, widowed, or abandoned, all of whom would've been vulnerable and in many cases shamed. He's talking to his people as a whole:

"Fear not, for you will not be ashamed;
    be not confounded, for you will not be disgraced;
for you will forget the shame of your youth,
    and the reproach of your widowhood you will remember no more.
For your Maker is your husband,
    the LORD of hosts is his name;
and the Holy One of Israel is your Redeemer,

the God of the whole earth he is called.
For the LORD has called you
like a wife deserted and grieved in spirit,
like a wife of youth when she is cast off,
says your God.
For a brief moment I deserted you,
but with great compassion I will gather you.
In overflowing anger for a moment
I hid my face from you,
but with everlasting love I will have compassion on you,"
says the LORD, your Redeemer. (Isa. 54:4–8)

This is one of many moments in the prophets when God presents himself as Israel's husband. The book of Hosea is built around this metaphor (see Hos. 2; cf. Jer. 2; 31; Ezek. 16). God is a faithful, loving husband. Israel is a cheating, reckless wife. Time and again, she abandons him for idols. Time and again, he woos her back. But the marriage never seems to work. Sinful people just can't live with a holy God.

Enter Jesus.

## THE BRIDEGROOM

My second visit to America was to celebrate a friend's wedding. A few years earlier, she had won a scholarship to study in the United Kingdom, and the scholars had been invited to a reception. As she walked up to the British embassy, a soldier was guarding the entrance. *That's the man I'm going to marry*, she thought. But then she shook herself. How would she even meet this guy? Later, she noticed the same man in the reception. He wasn't a guard. He was a Marine cadet on the same scholarship. She didn't tell him this story until their wedding day.

Few real-life love stories happen like this. For most, there is no writing in the sky. When Bryan and I were dating, he prayed for a sign that he should propose. He got nothing! But when Jesus walked onto the stage of human history, he made a bold and breathtaking claim. He said he was the bridegroom.

When the Pharisees complained that Jesus was eating and drinking with sinners, he replied that it wasn't the healthy who needed a doctor but the sick (Luke 5:31–32). Rather than realizing that they were sick, the Pharisees observed that his disciples didn't fast (Luke 5:33). "Can you make wedding guests fast," Jesus replied, "while the bridegroom is with them?" (Luke 5:34). John the Baptist spoke in similar terms:

> The one who has the bride is the bridegroom. The friend of the bridegroom, who stands and hears him, rejoices greatly at the bridegroom's voice. Therefore this joy of mine is now complete. (John 3:29)

Jesus is the bridegroom. He's come to claim God's wandering people. This first-century Jewish rabbi is stepping into the shoes of God almighty. Why? Because they fit. The cross is the dark room in which the image is developed. The resurrection blows it up. But just as each human is made in the image of God, albeit marred, each human marriage has the chance to reflect this great cosmic metaphor.

## HUSBANDS, LOVE YOUR WIVES AS CHRIST LOVED THE CHURCH

In my first year in college, I lived next door to a talented mathematician who was raised Hindu. We had many conversations about faith, and he started reading the Bible. But when God commanded Abraham to sacrifice his son in Genesis 22, my friend stopped. What kind of a God would do that? I urged him to read on. A few verses later, God stops Abraham the moment before he sacrifices Isaac and provides a ram instead. If my friend had read further in the Bible, he would've seen God sacrifice his beloved Son for us. Rather than seeing a cruel and heartless God, my friend would've seen his overflowing, sacrificial love. Stopping at Genesis 22:2 is like reading the first words of a note that says "I cannot bear you" and tearing it up before seeing the rest of the sentence: "being so far away." But in the same year that I told my friend he'd stopped too soon to see the overwhelming love of God, I'd made the same mistake myself.

When I first read Paul's instructions to wives, I was appalled:

> Wives, submit to your own husbands, as to the Lord. For the husband is
> the head of the wife even as Christ is head of the church, his body, and
> is himself its Savior. (Eph. 5:22–23)

For some time, I held this fragment of the letter in my hands, turning
it over and over, shocked by its misogynistic force. But then I started
to piece it together with what came next. "Husbands, love your wives
as Christ loved the church and gave himself up for her" (Eph. 5:25).
How did Christ love the church? By dying for her. By offering himself, naked and bleeding, on a Roman cross. By giving all he had to
meet her needs. By coming not to be served, but to serve and give his
life as a ransom for us. The complement to churchlike submission is
not chauvinistic rule. It's Christlike love and sacrifice. Husbands are
called four times to love their wives (Eph. 5:25, 28, 33; Col. 3:19) and
once to honor them (1 Pet. 3:7). Christian marriage is a negative held
up to the sun.

As Paul continues, we see that the point of human marriage *from
the very first* was to give us a picture of Jesus's love. Paul explains that
the "one flesh" union of husband and wife is truly fulfilled in Jesus and
his church:

> In the same way, husbands should love their wives as their own bodies.
> He who loves his wife loves himself. For no one ever hated his own
> flesh, but nourishes and cherishes it, just as Christ does the church,
> because we are members of his body. "Therefore a man shall leave his
> father and mother and hold fast to his wife, and the two shall become
> one flesh." This mystery is profound, and I am saying that it refers to
> Christ and the church. (Eph. 5:28–32)

Human marriage *at its very best* is a little, monochrome negative of
a massive wall print. Wives are not told to submit to their husbands
because women are worse at leading than men, but because the church
submits to Christ. Husbands are not told to give themselves up for
their wives because men are less valuable than women, but because

Jesus gave his life for us. Husbands are told to love their wives *as their own bodies*, because the church is Jesus's body on earth.

This signpost to Christ is why marriage is male and female, and why husbands and wives are called to different roles. Like Christ and the church, it's love across difference. Like Christ and the church, it's love built on sacrifice. Like Christ and the church, it's a flesh-uniting, life-creating, never-ending, exclusive love. Marriage is meant to point us to Christ.

But it's also meant to disappoint us.

## LOOK INTO YOUR EYES AND THE SKY'S THE LIMIT

In Act 1 of the musical *Hamilton*, Eliza remembers meeting Alexander Hamilton. As her sister was "dazzling the room," Hamilton walked in, and her heart went "Boom!" When Eliza looks into Hamilton's eyes, "the sky's the limit." She's drowning in them. Perhaps we've all felt moments like this. Our breath is knocked out of us by a sudden connection as we wonder, *Do they feel the same?* Eliza's love is requited: "If it takes fighting a war for us to meet," Hamilton says, "it will have been worth it." There is something ecstatic about falling in love. Responsiveness feels heavenly.

But as the plot of the play unfolds, we see this romance flounder. Hamilton swears to God that he will never leave Eliza feeling helpless. But he does. He has an affair that devastates her. And even before this, his obsession with his work leaves Eliza on the sidelines, craving his attention. What felt like a step into a dazzling new world became a stumble into heartbreak. By the end of the show, Hamilton is longing for Eliza's forgiveness: Forgiveness for his terrible affair; forgiveness for the death of their son; forgiveness for neglecting her as he pursued his love affair with work. Forgiveness.

What are we to make of this love story? Are we wrong to believe in the ecstasy of love? Not quite. If we take the Bible seriously, we will see that when romantic love consumes our hearts, when it makes us feel helpless, when it fills us with such joy that we can't think about anything else, and when it crushes us so cruelly we're lying in a pool of tears, it's pointing us to something else. It's giving us a picture of the one love that *can* last forever, the one romance that truly smashes through death, the love that, if we miss it now, will devastate us for all eternity. This lover invites each one of us to come to him.

In Revelation, John hears a great multitude proclaim, "the marriage of the Lamb has come, and his Bride has made herself ready" (Rev. 19:6–7), and we see Jesus's marriage to his church bringing heaven and earth back together (Rev. 21:1–3). This is the moment of ecstasy to which Christians are called. This is the lifetime of love into which we are eagerly invited. This is the wall-sized print that means we can throw away the negative. This is why Jesus says that there will be no human marriage in his new world (Matt. 22:30). It's not because human marriage isn't good, but because it will have been fulfilled. Just as Jesus is the sacrificial lamb to end all need for sacrifice, so he is the bridegroom who ends all need for human romance. In the TV comedy *The Good Place*, set in the afterlife, Chidi worries that he won't be able to keep his girlfriend Eleanor's interest through all eternity. He's right. No merely human lover could. But then, we aren't designed to. That role is taken by another man.

## WHAT ABOUT SAME-SEX SEXUALITY?

In the story of *Hamilton*, we glimpse passionate love between a man and a woman. But many other shows and songs reveal the passion of same-sex romance. In a moving scene in the classic British comedy *Four Weddings and a Funeral*, a gay character named Matthew reads a poem by W. H. Auden at his boyfriend Gareth's funeral:

> He was my North, my South, my East and West,
> My working week and my Sunday rest,
> My noon, my midnight, my talk, my song;
> I thought that love would last forever: I was wrong.

After Gareth's sudden death, the other main characters in the film, who are all single, realize that Gareth and Matthew had effectively been married all along. This film came out 20 years before gay marriage was legalized in Britain. But like many films and songs before and since, it fleshes out the claim that love is love: that a same-sex romance can be just as faithful, deep, and enduring as a heterosexual one, and therefore same-sex couples should be able to marry. What does the Bible say about this?

When she was first exploring Christianity, my friend Rachel asked some lesbian friends this question. Rachel had grown up in a non-Christian home. At 15, she'd fallen for a beautiful senior girl. They became close friends, and when this girl asked Rachel what she wanted for her 16th birthday, she asked her for a kiss. This began an on-and-off sexual relationship that lasted into college—despite various other relationships that convinced Rachel she was generally into girls, not guys. When Rachel was accepted into Yale, it seemed like all her dreams were coming true. But in the winter of her freshman year, her girlfriend left her.

In small-town California, Rachel had been a cheerful atheist. This attitude had translated well to student life at Yale. But in her misery at losing the woman she loved, Rachel heard a lecture on Descartes with a supposed proof for God. She found the argument unconvincing, but somehow it made her curious. She'd always laughed at Christianity. It seemed intellectually weak, and she'd discovered that the pretty Christian girls at her high school were easy to seduce, despite their supposed morals. But as Rachel became interested and started googling religious terms, she kept stumbling upon Jesus. She found him surprisingly attractive. And yet she'd picked up from the culture that Christians didn't approve of gay relationships, so she asked the only self-identifying Christians she knew at Yale—a lesbian couple—what they thought.

Rachel's friends told her it was all a big misunderstanding: if you read the Bible rightly, it *doesn't* reject same-sex marriage. But when Rachel read the passages they claimed to explain, she was bitterly disappointed. She was no Bible scholar, but she was good at reading books. She'd wondered if this strange religion based on this intriguing first-century Jew had room for someone like her. But the Bible's "No" to gay relationships was unmistakable. It felt like a door had been opened a crack and then shut in her face.

Rachel ended up walking through that door nonetheless. Jesus's offer of love was too good to turn down, whatever the cost. Now, she reads the Bible in its original Greek and Hebrew, and is studying for a PhD in theology. Nothing she's learned in the last 16 years has changed the conclusion she drew when she first read the texts. She now sees the beautiful, wall-sized print of Jesus's love, but the sharp lines in the negative remain.[1]

My story is different from Rachel's. I've been a Christian for as long as I can remember, and I've been drawn to women for that long too. When I was 25, I met an empathetic Christian man, who knew my story and loved me nonetheless. When gay marriage became legal in America, we'd been happily married for eight years. But I hadn't told even my closest friends about my ongoing experience of same-sex attraction. I was desperately afraid it would make them want to take a step back: not in outright rejection, but in discomfort.

At the same time, it broke my heart that my non-believing friends thought Christianity was hateful. Without quite coming out on Facebook, I explained why I hadn't turned my profile picture rainbow. One secular Jewish friend asked why Christians pick and choose among biblical commands. If I was OK with eating shellfish (which the Old Testament prohibits) I should also be OK with gay relationships (which the Old Testament also prohibits). I explained that the Old Testament law isn't binding on Christians, because it has been fulfilled in Christ, and that while the New Testament clearly affirms that Christians can eat all kinds of foods, it clearly prohibits same-sex sex. But in my heart, I wanted to say that if I'd been picking and choosing while exploring what the Bible said, I'd gladly have given up shrimp to marry a woman!

So was I wrong in my reading?

## FOLLOW THE BRUSHSTROKES

Some argue that even if the New Testament seems to say "No" to same-sex sex, if we look at the big picture of how the New Testament relates to the Old, we'll see that it pushes us toward affirming gay marriage. They suggest that the scriptural trajectory toward love and inclusion is like the sweep of a brushstroke, so even if the brush has left the canvas, we can see where it was moving and continue the

---

1.    You can read more about Rachel's testimony in her excellent book, *Born Again This Way: Coming Out, Coming to Faith, and What Comes Next* (Charlotte, NC: The Good Book Co., 2020).

stroke. But if we look closely at the passages that prohibit gay relationships, we'll find they already fit with the broad brushstrokes of the
biblical picture.

In the Old Testament, as we have seen, God's relationship with his
people is pictured as a marriage, and worshiping other gods as infidel-
ity. Idolatry equals adultery. In Romans 1:21–27, Paul sticks with this
theme, weaving between idolatry and sexual sin, and arguing that sexual immorality in general, and homosexual relationships in particular,
are a consequence of people turning from God. This does not mean
that an individual's experience of same-sex *attraction* results from rejecting God. Most Christians struggle at times with attractions that,
if followed, would lead them into sexual sin. In this respect, we're all
in the same boat. But if the faithful one-flesh union of a man and a
woman pictures Christ's marriage to his church, any sexual relationship outside that model pictures idolatry. Without boundary lines,
there is no image.

The New Testament "No" to same-sex sexuality is drawn in char-
coal on the biblical big picture, but all other forms of sexual immorality are also sharply excluded. Whenever Paul mentions same-sex
sexual sin, he also talks about other forms of sin—sexual and otherwise. In Romans 1:28–32, he lists greed, envy, murder, strife, deceit,
malice, disobedience to parents, lack of understanding, lack of faithfulness, lack of love, and lack of mercy as other fruits of turning away
from God. Similarly, in 1 Corinthians 6:9–11, Paul lists idol worship,
adultery, theft, greed, drunkenness, slandering, and swindling alongside both heterosexual and homosexual sin. And strikingly, in 1 Timothy 1:10, Paul lists the sin of enslaving people right next to the sin of
homosexual sex.

Sometimes people argue that Paul supported slavery as much as
he condemned gay relationships, and since we no longer listen to Paul
on slavery, we should not listen to him on homosexuality. But while
Paul gave slaves (who formed a significant proportion of the early
church) instructions on how to live well for Jesus in their situation,
and called masters to treat their slaves well, because their master in
heaven was watching (Eph. 5:9), the idea that Paul supported slavery
falls apart in multiple places. One key text is Paul's letter to Philemon,
when he calls an enslaved man, Onesimus, his "son" (Philem. 1:10) and

his "very heart" (Philem. 1:12). Paul urges Onesimus's former master to welcome him back no longer as a slave but as a "beloved brother" and to receive him as he would receive Paul, Philemon's most respected mentor (Philem. 1:17). This letter totally upends the master-slave relationship. Meanwhile, in Paul's letter to Timothy, we see a clear condemnation of the very sin on which chattel slavery in America was based.

Paul's catalog of sinful practices in 1 Timothy 1:8–10 is built on the Ten Commandments of Exodus 20. The fifth commandment, "Honor your father and your mother," pairs with "those who strike their fathers and mothers." The sixth commandment, "You shall not murder," pairs with "murderers." The seventh, "You shall not commit adultery," pairs with both "the sexually immoral" and "men who practice homosexuality." And the eighth commandment, "You shall not steal," pairs with "enslavers." Stealing human beings to enslave them is the worst kind of stealing. It was punishable under the Old Testament law by death (Ex. 21:16). There is no doubt from his writings that if Paul had witnessed the race-based, man-stealing, chattel slavery practiced by self-identifying Christians in America he would have condemned it outright. But he would also have condemned the ways in which many churches today condone sexual immorality for Christians, both heterosexual and homosexual.

Is this because Paul was a homophobic bigot with a self-righteous, hateful heart? No. Right after the passage in which he lists gay sex among other forms of sin, Paul writes, "The saying is trustworthy and deserving of full acceptance, that Christ Jesus came into the world to save sinners, of whom I am the foremost" (1 Tim. 1:15). Paul doesn't look down on people in gay relationships from a moral high ground. He says he is the worst sinner he knows, saved only to prove that someone so bad could be redeemed (1 Tim. 1:16). And every time Paul writes about same-sex sexual sin, he reminds his readers they are sinners too. In Romans 2, anyone who has read Paul's list of sins and come out feeling smug gets a slap in the face: "You, therefore, have no excuse, you who pass judgement on someone else, for at whatever point you judge another, you are condemning yourself" (Rom. 2:1). In 1 Corinthians 6, the apostle's words are more tender. After listing various sins, including gay sex, he reminds his readers, "And such were

some of you. But you were washed, you were sanctified, you were justified in the name of the Lord Jesus Christ and by the Spirit of God"
(1 Cor. 6:11). This verse proves that some of the first Christians, like my
friend Rachel, came to Christ with a history of gay relationships, and
that they were made holy by the blood of Christ just like anyone else.

Some argue that Paul didn't realize there could be mutual love and
devotion between people in a same-sex romance, because he only saw
promiscuous and exploitative models of homosexual relationships (for
example, adult men with teenage boys, or sex with male slaves). They
say he would have affirmed gay marriage if he'd known there was such
a possibility. But while gay marriage was by no means common in the
ancient world, it was not unheard of. In fact, the notorious emperor
Nero, who ruled Rome at the time when Paul was writing, married
other men on two separate occasions. As historian and queer studies
pioneer Louis Crompton puts it, "Nowhere does Paul or any other
Jewish writer of this period imply the least acceptance of same-sex
relations under any circumstances." In fact, "The idea that homosex-
uals might be redeemed by mutual devotion would have been wholly
foreign to Paul or any other Jew or early Christian."[2]

But does this mean God's Word is against same-sex love? Not
at all.

## SENDING YOU MY VERY HEART

The Bible calls us repeatedly to non-erotic same-sex love. While one-
flesh union is reserved for marriage, all Christians are "one body"
together (e.g. 1 Cor. 12:12–27; Rom. 12:4–5; Eph. 4:4). Paul writes of
Christians being "knit together in love" because they are "knit together" in Christ's body (Col. 2:2, 19). He says he was among the Thessa-
lonians "like a nursing mother with her children" (1 Thess. 2:7), and he
"yearns for" the Philippians "with the affection of Christ Jesus" (Phil.
1:8). Paul's letters to the churches are in the truest sense love letters.

Paul also talks in the most intimate terms about his love for individual believers. He calls Epaphroditus his "brother and co-worker

2.   Louis Crompton, *Homosexuality and Civilization* (Cambridge, MA: Harvard University Press, 2003), 114.

and fellow soldier" (Phil. 2:25), evoking the deep bond that builds between soldiers, as they have each other's backs. But Paul's most affectionate language for another individual comes in his letter to Philemon. Onesimus and Paul had met in prison. They had become gospel partners. Paul now calls Onesimus his child (Philem. 10) and tells Philemon he is sending him his "very heart" (Philem. 12).

One of the cultural adjustments I had to make when I moved to the United States was that Americans say "I love you" much more freely. At first, it felt awkward, even hollow. Those words are used sparingly in England, so I bristled when friends declared their love, especially if we weren't that close. But after 12 years in America, I often say those words to friends. When backed with a true heart commitment, a true willingness to sacrifice for each other, a true affection that goes beyond mere friendliness, I now believe they draw us closer to New Testament norms. And while the boundaries on sexual touching are clear, the Bible calls Christians to physical expressions of mutual affection in Christ: the command "Greet one another with a holy kiss" appears five times (Rom. 16:16; 1 Cor. 16:20; 2 Cor. 13:12; 1 Thess. 5:26; 1 Pet. 5:14).

"By this all people will know that you are my disciples," Jesus said, "if you have love for one another" (John 13:35) We see this intimacy in Jesus's same-sex relationships. John refers to himself as "the one whom Jesus loved" (John 20:2). Some have tried to argue that Jesus's relationship with John was homoerotic. But while "love" in English is one size fits all, the Greek word John uses is not the word commonly used for sexual love. John also writes of Jesus loving Lazarus (John 11:3) and records a conversation between Jesus and Peter after Jesus's resurrection, in which Jesus asks Peter three times if he loves him, and Peter replies three times that he does (John 21:15–17). Like sibling love and friend love, the love between same-sex believers is precious, deep, and intimate. But it's not sexual, and it's not exclusive.

I recently watched an episode of *Planet Earth* in which a baby elephant was separated from its mother in a sandstorm. The herd was on a long, exhausting trek to find water, and after the sandstorm, the lonely child had picked up its mother's tracks. But as the camera panned out on this solitary calf, the narrator told us the painful truth: this calf was following its mother's tracks in the wrong direction.

It's not that the Bible doesn't celebrate same-sex love. It does. But rather than pointing us toward exclusive, sexual relationships, these scriptural tracks lead to non-erotic, non-exclusive bonds between believers. Correctly followed, these tracks lead to a waterhole of love-filled life in Christ. But turned to sexual sin, they lead to death.

Looking at other biblical snapshots will help us understand.

## SNAPSHOTS OF LOVE

Not long ago I saw a video posted on Twitter of a dad playing a guitar and singing the Elvis Presley's hit "Can't Help Falling in Love." More than a million people had watched the video—not because the man was a great singer, but because he was singing to his newborn son. No one would think this dad was expressing sexual love. If we'd thought that, we would be repulsed. But it was a love song nonetheless, and this man's use of a romantic song to express his feelings for his newborn son was moving because it showed us that a completely *non-romantic* love can be just as deep as a romantic one.

If we look back through the film of Scripture, we'll find fatherly love is a powerful picture of God's love. Just as the best human marriages give us a glimpse of Jesus's love for us, so in the best human fathers we see a snapshot of God's paternal love. The Bible also uses maternal metaphors for God, who says he gave birth to Israel and compares himself to a nursing mother (e.g., Deut. 32:18; Isa. 45:15). So, in the best of human mothers, we bathe in the warmth of God's motherly love.

Parental relationships are vital. But they are vitally different from sexual relationships. Adding a sexual element to parental love is like dropping lemon into milk: it spoils it instantly. This isn't because sex is bad, or because parental love is bad. From God's perspective, both are *very* good. But sex doesn't belong in parent-child relationships. Both marriage and parenthood depict God's love for us. But superimposing one image on the other ruins both. The Bible says the same about same-sex love: like sexual love and parental love, it's a spoke in the wheel of human love that occupies its own unique and precious space and helps us understand another aspect of God's love for us.

In our culture today, it's easy to believe that sexual love is the peak of human intimacy, followed closely by parental love. Within this mentality, it's easy for Christians to believe that the nuclear family is the locus for all real, lasting love. But Jesus torpedoes this idea: "Greater love has no one than this," Jesus declares, "that he lay down his life for his friends" (John 15:13). According to Jesus, friendship isn't the poor cousin of romantic love. Self-sacrificing friendship love is just as good as any other kind.

Rather than prizing the nuclear family above all, Jesus stressed the family of the church. One day, while he was teaching, Jesus heard that his mother and brothers were waiting to speak with him. He replied, "Who is my mother, and who are my brothers?" Pointing to his disciples, he said, "Here are my mother and my brothers. For whoever does the will of my Father in heaven is my brother and sister and mother" (Matt. 12:46–50). Jesus isn't denigrating the nuclear family. He's setting it in its proper context: the blood-bought brotherhood and sisterhood of the church.

This is the context in which Paul lived as a single man and commended singleness even over marriage (1 Cor. 7:32–35, 40). This is the context in which same-sex-attracted Christians should be living today: a loving family of faith, in which lives and food and struggles with sin are shared between siblings in Christ. I used to fear that sharing my experience of same-sex attraction with my Christian friends would cause them to take a half-step back from me. Now I realize that by *not* sharing my struggles, I was taking a half-step back from them. For same-sex-attracted Christians, the struggle can be very real. When my friend Rachel fell back into a sexual relationship with another girl, it was the love of her Christian friends that helped her turn around. The person who leaves a gay relationship to fall into the arms of Christ should feel more love, not less. The arms of those who are Jesus's body here on earth should be his tangible embrace.

Last summer, I did a Q&A for students alongside a single pastor many years my senior. We were each asked what we'd tell ourselves at 18. The pastor said that at 18, he was painfully aware of his same-sex attraction and deeply afraid he wouldn't be able to live long-term without pursuing it. Decades later, his patterns of attraction haven't changed. But he wanted to tell his 18-year-old self just how good and full of love his life would be.

## LET'S BE MORE BIBLICAL, NOT LESS

Some argue that for the church to survive in a love-is-love world, we must become less biblical. I think the opposite is true. For far too long, we've bought the lie that marriage is the ultimate good. For far too long, we've bought the lie that singleness is second-best. For far too long we've undervalued same-sex love and bought the lie that the nuclear family is more important than the church.

Christian marriage at its best is a beautiful picture of Jesus's love for us. But it's not the only one. "By this we know love," John writes, "that [Jesus] laid down his life for us, and we ought to lay down our lives for the brothers" (1 John 3:16). In Christ we are one body together, brothers and sisters, comrades in arms, knit together in love. If Christians lived like this, the plague of loneliness would be over, and all of us—single or married, same-sex attracted or straight, old or young, widowed or newlywed—would be embraced into a family. These are the first tremors of the earthquake of God's love that will remake the world when Jesus returns.

When I left the coffee shop in Missouri, I hugged the women I'd been talking with, and we laughed together. But they warned me that nothing I had said had changed their support for the next day's protest. Afterward on Twitter, one of the women said kindly that she felt sorry for me that I had "never experienced love and passion with another woman." I texted my friend Rachel, who replied, "She's wrong about the love."

# 3

# "THE GAY-RIGHTS MOVEMENT IS THE NEW CIVIL-RIGHTS MOVEMENT"

"Can you untangle this for me?"

My daughter's hands were filled with wool. She wanted to start a project, but two different colors were twisted together. It had reached the point that if you pulled on any one thread, the knot grew tighter. So I started the slow, careful, painstaking process of teasing the various knots apart. Every time I seemed to be making progress and was winding one color neatly round my hand, I'd come to the end of the thread. It turned out she'd been extracting wool by pulling on random ends and then cutting the thread when she came to a knot.

In chapter 1, we explored the biblical big picture of love and unity across racial and cultural difference. In chapter 2, we saw the biblical big picture of sex and marriage and how the Bible has a different beautiful vision for same-sex relationships. In this chapter we'll examine how the historic failure of white Christians to love their black neighbors has propelled the powerful claim that the gay-rights movement is the new civil-rights movement. This is the tape that tethers "love is love" to "black lives matter." We'll look at why this claim is so persuasive, as well as why it ultimately fails. And we'll see that short-cuts only make the slow, careful, painstaking process of untangling this knot more difficult.

## 'YOU'RE ON THE WRONG SIDE OF HISTORY'

On November 14, 1960, a 6-year-old girl named Ruby Bridges was escorted into an elementary school in New Orleans. The year Ruby was born, the U.S. Supreme Court had ruled public school segregation unconstitutional. But many were still resisting integration. This brave 6-year-old's small steps into William Frantz Elementary School were part of an attempted giant leap for America: a leap toward educating black and white children together, a leap toward equality, a leap toward the day when "little black boys and black girls will be able to join hands with little white boys and white girls as sisters and brothers."[1] But rather than joining with this great leap, many white parents took another step. When Ruby Bridges entered school, she faced death threats, racist slurs, and a white crowd chanting, "2-4-6-8, we don't want to integrate." Five hundred white children were pulled from school that day, and as more and more schools became integrated, many white parents moved their children to segregated private schools.

Today, we're all appalled by this behavior. But those of us who are Christians should be more appalled. Many of the all-white private schools had "Christian" or "church" in their name. It wasn't just that white parents didn't want their children in integrated schools. White *Christian* parents didn't want it. These "segregation academies" are one example among many in American history of when white Christians have sided *against* love across racial difference. Not every white Christian, to be sure, but far too many.

Today, when people see Christian opposition to gay marriage, they think it's just the same song, second verse. The reasoning runs like this:

---

1.   Martin Luther King Jr., "I Have a Dream" speech delivered at the March on Washington for Jobs and Freedom, August 28, 1963, https://www.americanrhetoric.com/speeches/mlkihavead-ream.htm.

just as Christians have oppressed and terrorized African Americans, so Christians have oppressed and terrorized gay and lesbian people. Just as we are now ashamed of 1960s segregationists, so one day our descendants will be ashamed of us, if we continue to oppose gay marriage. I recently read a *New York Times* column titled "Choosing The Right Side Of History" in which Pulitzer Prize–winning journalist Nicholas Kristof made the usual move to tie gay rights to civil rights.[2] Those who oppose any progressive ideal, he argues, are on the wrong side of history. As the Rev. Dr. Martin Luther King Jr. declared, "The arc of the moral universe is long, but it bends toward justice."[3]

Given the history of white Christian racism, I can see why people think Christianity is the problem. In the minds of many of my secular friends, if we're going to become more just, we must become less biblical. Perhaps a progressive form of Christianity can survive in the modern world. But traditional, Bible-based Christian faith—the kind that cannot affirm gay marriage—has failed. The gay-rights movement picked up the torch of the civil-rights movement and ran. We must run with it or be left behind. Or so the thinking holds.

But there are multiple problems with this perspective.

First, as we saw in chapter 1, without the God of the Bible, our ideals of human equality and justice have no foundation. Thus Yuval Noah Harari declares, "There are no gods in the universe, no nations, no money, no human rights, no laws, and no justice outside the common imagination of human beings."[4] From an atheist perspective, there's no reason to believe in human rights, no basis for love across difference, and no meaning to right and wrong beyond our shared imagination at a certain time. If this is true, then race-based slavery and segregation laws were not absolutely *wrong*. So long as they were right according to the "shared imagination" of enough people at the time, that's good enough, because there is no universal, timeless

2.   Nicholas Kristof, "Choosing The Right Side Of History," *The New York Times*, October 14, 2020, A27, https://www.nytimes.com/2020/10/14/opinion/amy-coney-barrett-health-care. html. The online version modified the title: "Will We Choose the Right Side of History?"

3.   Martin Luther King Jr., "Out of the Long Night of Segregation," *Missions: An International Baptist Magazine*, February 8, 1958, https://thekingcenter.org/archive/document/out-long-night-segregation.

4.   Harari, *Sapiens*, 28.

moral standard. As Richard Dawkins puts it, "moral values are 'in the air' and they change from century to century, even from decade to decade."[5] The very idea of human rights is, as Harari argues, a Christian invention. So we need Christianity to be *right* for human-rights abuses to be *wrong*.

Second, the idea that minorities should be protected, not oppressed, also came to us from Christianity. As historian Tom Holland points out, such protection would have seemed quite strange in the first-century Greco-Roman empire in which Christianity was born, where the ethic was essentially this: "The strong do what they have the power to do. The weak must suck it up."[6] But when a poor man from a historically oppressed racial and religious group claimed to be God in human flesh, commanded love for society's most vulnerable and died a slave's death on a Roman cross, he made the poor, oppressed, and victimized forever central to God's moral plan.

Third, without belief in a creator God, there *is* no story to the universe. When King asserted that the arc of the moral universe bends toward justice, he said it *because* he was a Christian, who believed in Jesus's death and resurrection:

> Evil may so shape events that Caesar will occupy a palace and Christ a cross, but that same Christ will rise up and split history into A.D. and B.C., so that even the life of Caesar must be dated by his name. Yes, "the arc of the moral universe is long, but it bends toward justice."[7]

If there is no God who made the universe, there is no moral universe to bend. There is, as Dawkins puts it, "no design, no purpose, no evil and no good, nothing but blind, pitiless indifference."[8] If there is no justice-loving God who made the world, there's no reason to believe the world will finally be just. In fact, there's no way of even knowing what that would mean.

5.   Richard Dawkins, *Outgrowing God: A Beginner's Guide* (New York: Random House, 2019), 159.
6.   See Holland, *Dominion*, 41. Quoting from Thucydides, 5.89.
7.   Martin Luther King Jr., "Out of the Long Night of Segregation," *Missions: An International Baptist Magazine*, February 8, 1958.
8.   Richard Dawkins, *A River Out of Eden: A Darwinian View of Life* (New York: Basic Books, 1996), 133.

Fourth, the problem with Christians who supported segregation was not that they listened to the Bible too much, but too little. While the Bible cuts firmly against gay marriage for believers, it cuts equally firmly in favor of racial equality and integration. Repenting of racial injustice means turning back to the Bible. Affirming gay marriage for believers means turning away. In the time before abolition, slaveholders often either stopped those they enslaved from reading the Bible at all, or drastically edited it. As Esau McCaulley puts it, "Part of them knew that their exegetical conclusions could only be maintained if the enslaved were denied firsthand experience of the text."[9] It takes as much careful editing to make the Bible seem like it supports segregation as to make it seem like it affirms gay marriage. In both cases, it's like editing a "Do Not Enter" sign by crossing out "Do Not."

The fifth problem with the claim that Christians who don't affirm gay marriage for believers are on the wrong side of history is that (in purely demographic terms) it seems unlikely to be true. Today, 31 percent of the world identifies as Christian, and that proportion is set to increase slightly to 32 percent by 2060, while the proportion of the world not affiliated with any religion is set to decline from 16 percent to 13 percent.[10] Christianity's closest global competitor is Islam, which is set to grow from 24 percent to 31 percent and which also does not affirm gay marriage. Many expected progressive Christianity that affirms gay marriage to thrive while Bible-based faith declined. But across North America, mainline churches have seen a steep decline while evangelical churches have fared much better.[11] Globally, evangelical and Pentecostal churches (mostly composed of believers of color) are growing, while more liberal churches (mostly composed of white people) are declining.

9.  McCaulley, *Reading While Black*, 170.
10. See "The Future of World Religions: Population Growth Projections, 2010–2050," Pew Research Center, April 2, 2015, http://www.pewforum.org/2015/04/02/religious-projections-2010-2050, and "Projected Change in Global Population, 2015–2060," Pew Research Center, March 31, 2017, http://www.pewforum.org/2017/04/05/the-changing-global-religiouslandscape/pf_17-04-05_projectionsupdate_changepopulation640px.
11. "The Changing Religious Composition of the U.S.," in America's Changing Religious Landscape, Pew Research Center, May 12, 2015, http://www.pewforum.org/2015/05/12/chapter-1-the-changing-religious-composition-of-the-u-s/.

Finally, the claim that anyone who opposes gay marriage for Christians is equivalent to a '60s segregationist fails when we look at the actual beliefs of black Americans.

## AWKWARD VIEWS OF BLACK AMERICANS

In 2001, roughly a third of American adults supported same-sex marriage. By 2013, it was half. When gay marriage was legalized across the country in 2015, 55 percent of Americans agreed. Since then, support has grown further, with 61 percent of Americans affirming gay marriage in 2019.[12] This change in a single generation is one of the most remarkable cultural shifts of our age. It's important to note that someone could oppose gay marriage *for believers* while not thinking it should be against the law. As a comparison, I believe that frequent prayer, weekly church attendance (except in extreme circumstances), generous giving to those in need, and living as either faithfully single or faithfully married are vital for Christian discipleship. But I don't think they should be enforced by law. I believe that Christian ethics are most attractive when they are undertaken freely. Still, to the extent that not believing gay marriage should be legal is some kind of proxy to underlying beliefs, we see a significant difference between black and white Americans.

In many people's minds, the fact that gay marriage was legalized across all states under America's first black president solidified the idea that the gay-rights movement is the natural heir of the civil-rights movement. But while President Obama supported the change, at the time only 39 percent of black Americans agreed. By 2019, only 51 percent of black Americans supported same-sex marriage versus 62 percent of whites.[13] This difference is the more remarkable as the average age of black Americans is younger than whites, and younger people

12.   Numbers quoted from "Changing attitudes on same-sex marriage," Pew Research Center, May 14, 2019, https://www.pewforum.org/fact-sheet/changing-attitudes-on-gay-marriage. A Gallup poll found slightly higher levels of support, but a similar trajectory across time: https://news.gallup.com/poll/311672/support-sex-marriage-matches-record-high.aspx.

13.   "Changing attitudes on same-sex marriage," 2019.

are more likely to support gay marriage.[14] Moreover, black Americans are far more likely to vote Democrat, and Democrats are far more likely than Republicans to support gay marriage.[15]

So, what keeps so many black Americans from affirming gay marriage? There are likely several factors. One is that Americans with college degrees are far more likely to support same-sex marriage than those with high-school degrees or less, and African Americans have historically had less access to higher education.[16] But another significant factor is the much higher levels of Christian faith and practice among black Americans.[17]

As we saw in chapter 1, black Americans are more likely to identify as Christians than their white peers are. They poll higher on every measure of Christian practice and tend to be theologically conservative.[18] While black Protestants considered as a whole (without separating theological progressives from conservatives) are significantly less likely than white evangelicals to oppose gay marriage, they are far more likely than white mainline Protestants to do so.[19] Whichever way you read it, the fact that nearly half of all black Americans *still* do not support gay marriage is a major problem for the claim that the gay-rights movement is the new civil-rights movement. It certainly discredits the idea that anyone who does not support gay

14. In 2019, 83 percent of Americans age 18 to 29 supported gay marriage versus only 47 percent of those 65 and older.

15. In 2019, 79 percent of Democrats supported gay marriage versus only 44 percent of Republicans.

16. In 2016, 68 percent of Americans with a college degree said same-sex marriage should be legal versus 45 percent of those without. Hannah Fingerhut, "Support steady for same-sex marriage and acceptance of homosexuality," Pew Research Center, May 12, 2016, https://www.pewresearch.org/fact-tank/2016/05/12/support-steady-for-same-sex-marriage-and-acceptance-of-homosexuality.

17. For a discussion of this from 2015, when same-sex marriage was being considered by the U.S. Supreme Court, see Frank Newport, "Religion, Race, and Same-Sex Marriage," Gallup Blog, May 1, 2015, https://news.gallup.com/opinion/polling-matters/182978/religion-race-sex-marriage.aspx.

18. The faith statements of the largest black protestant denominations testify to this.

19. A 2020 survey found that 34 percent of white evangelicals supported gay marriage versus 57 percent of black Protestants and 79 percent of white mainline Protestants. See "Dueling Realities: Amid Multiple Crises, Trump and Biden Supporters See Different Priorities and Futures for the Nation," Public Religion Research Institute, October 19, 2020, https://www.prri.org/research/amid-multiple-crises-trump-and-biden-supporters-see-different-realities-and-futures-for-the-nation.

marriage for religious reasons is like a '60s segregationist. Of course, you could say that black Christians are just wrong about gay marriage. But minimally, this divergence of views shows that we cannot lump the interests and beliefs of all minorities together. We see this crack in the supposedly cohesive shell of diversity most clearly when failure to affirm gay relationships leads to discrimination against black people in white-majority countries.

In 2019, a black actress named Seyi Omooba was fired from starring in a London production of *The Color Purple* because of a 2014 Facebook post in which she expressed her Christian beliefs about gay relationships.[20] "I just quoted what the Bible says about homosexuality," Omooba explained, "the need for repentance, but ultimately God's love for all humanity."[21] The firing of a black woman because she holds traditionally Christian views is not a triumph for diversity. Quite the reverse.

The fact that many black people in the United States do not affirm gay relationships is hinted at in the mission statement of Black Lives Matter. The second point in that mission statement says:

> We affirm the lives of Black queer and trans folks, disabled folks, undocumented folks, folks with records, women, and all Black lives along the gender spectrum. Our network centers those who have been marginalized within Black liberation movements.

Of course, Christians should affirm and defend the right to a life free from harassment, bullying, and violence for any person as an image-bearer of God. Black people who identify as queer or trans matter so much to Jesus that he came to die for them, and any hatred and abuse poured out on LGBT+ people by Christians goes quite against Christ's call to love our neighbor as ourself. But the acknowledgement that LGBT+ people have been "marginalized within Black liberation movements" shows that the gay-rights movement is not smoothly

20.  Sofia Lotto Persio, "The Color Purple actress under fire over anti-gay post," *Pink News*, March 17, 2019, https://www.pinknews.co.uk/2019/03/17/the-colour-purple-actress-anti-gay-post.

21.  Jonathan Ames, "Seyi Omooba: Actress fired for anti-gay Facebook message wins backing in legal fight," *The Times*, November 16, 2020, https://www.thetimes.co.uk/article/seyi-omooba-actress-fired-for-anti-gay-facebook-message-wins-backing-in-legal-fight-srczzfj67.

continuous with the civil-rights movement. Most African Americans engaged in the civil-rights movement would not have affirmed gay relationships or transgender identities and (ironically) the people most likely to hold progressive views on LGBT+ rights today are white and economically privileged.

Race, sexual choices, and gender identities are different threads that must be untangled to be understood. As we look more closely at the comparison people make between being born gay and being born black, we'll find intrinsic problems that ultimately don't do justice to people in either group.

We see this most clearly when gay marriage is compared to interracial marriage.

## IS GAY MARRIAGE LIKE INTERRACIAL MARRIAGE?

In 1967, the U.S. Supreme Court overturned laws banning interracial marriage. The case at hand was that of Mildred and Richard Loving, who had both been sentenced to prison for a year. Richard was white. Mildred was part African American and part Native American. Their marriage violated Virginia state law. It's shocking to think how recent this is and to think that, despite all that the Bible says about love across racial and cultural difference, many Christians insisted that interracial marriage violated God's plan.

When the Supreme Court was considering the case for gay marriage in 2015, *Loving v. Virginia* was cited as a precedent. The court voted 5 to 4 in favor. Justice Clarence Thomas—the only African American justice on the court—was one of the four who argued against same-sex marriage. But whatever the rights and wrongs of the U.S. legal system, is it right to see gay marriage as a natural heir to mixed-race marriage? I don't think so.

For centuries, motivated by racism, white scientists claimed that there were meaningful biological differences between black people and white people. But they were wrong. In fact, now that we can analyze each human's DNA, we can see that there is often more genetic variation between two people of African descent than between a black person and a white person. What's more, any apparent differences between an individual black person and a white person—skin color or hair type, for example—are irrelevant when it comes to having sex and having kids. While the laws against interracial marriage in the United States were partly based on the claim by scientists in the mid-19th century that racial mixing led to infertility, this claim was completely false.[22] Nothing about interracial marriage changes what marriage was designed to be: a picture of Jesus's love for the church and a partnership for bearing and raising children.

The case of same-sex marriage is different. There are significant biological differences between men and women. In many life situations, such differences don't matter. For example, to do most jobs, it doesn't matter if you're male or female. But the differences between men and women are highly relevant in marriage. In fact, this is the setting in which they're *most* relevant, because the differences enable us to have babies together. Equating same-sex marriage to mixed-race marriage only works if you accept the wrong beliefs about people from different racial backgrounds that white scientists used to peddle. This doesn't by itself mean gay marriage is wrong. But it does mean we can't say it's the natural successor to mixed-race marriage.

## IS BEING GAY LIKE BEING BLACK?

The gay-rights movement built on the foundation of the civil-rights movement on the basis that being gay was in important respects like being black. Each of us is born with an unchosen racial heritage. Likewise, the pioneers of gay rights argued, some people are born gay. They should, therefore, have the same right as anyone else to work in any job, serve in the military, and marry. But there are two substantial problems with the analogy.

First, when people compare being gay to being black, they typically don't distinguish between a person's *attractions* and *actions*. Whatever our patterns of attraction, we don't *choose* our attractions. I didn't choose, for example, to be attracted to women. But we do choose our actions, and we all agree that sexual actions carry moral weight. For

22. William H. Tucker, "The Ideology of Racism: Misusing Science to Justify Racial Discrimination," UN Chronicle, https://www.un.org/en/chronicle/article/ideology-racism-misusing-science-justify-racial-discrimination.

example, not long ago I met a man in his 50s who has wrestled all his married life with attraction to other women. He has worked hard to turn away from these attractions. But he could have made other choices. When attracted to another woman, he could've responded by starting an affair. He could've divorced his wife to marry another woman. Or he could have attempted a sexual assault. All of these are moral decisions, and all of us would agree that the last choice at least would be immoral. In each case, the attraction is the same, but the action is different. My friend experiences attraction, and then he makes moral choices about how he responds. Likewise, while my same-sex attraction is as unchosen as the color of my skin, if I left my husband for another woman and then said I had no choice but to do so, I'd be denying a basic fact of my humanity: that I'm a human who makes moral decisions, not an animal who simply responds to her drives. When you think about it, it's dehumanizing not to distinguish between someone's attractions and actions.

Second, while racial heritage is both unchosen and unchanging, the latest research shows that our sexual attractions can change over time, and that bisexuality is far more common than exclusive same-sex sexuality. University of Utah professor Lisa Diamond, who identifies as a lesbian, is a pioneer of this research. Diamond has found that women like me, who experience same-sex attraction but not exclusively, are by far the largest group of same-sex attracted people. About 14 percent of women experience attraction to other women, while only 1 percent are never attracted to men. For men, it's roughly 7 percent who are attracted to other men, while only 2 percent are never attracted to women. This means there is significant complexity within labeled categories. For example, 42 percent of self-identified lesbians and 31 percent of self-identified gay men report having had an opposite-sex sexual fantasy in the last year, one study found.[23]

---

23. Professor Diamond summarizes her data in a lecture at Cornell University, "Just How Different Are Female and Male Sexual Orientation?," YouTube, October 17, 2013, https://www.youtube.com/watch?v=m2rTHDOuUBw. For a short summary on the different proportions of the population that report same-sex attraction, same-sex sexual behavior, and LGBT identity, see Gary J. Gates, "How Many People are Lesbian, Gay, Bisexual, and Transgender?," UCLA School of Law, Williams Institute, April 2011, https://williamsinstitute.law.ucla.edu/publications/how-many-people-lgbt.

Popular culture is starting to acknowledge this complexity. The Canadian comedy *Schitt's Creek* won a raft of Emmys in 2020. One of its central characters, David, signals gay identity from the start and ends up marrying another man. But in the first season, the show plays with the audience's expectations by having David sleep with a woman and say he's bisexual. Meanwhile, the man whom David finally marries was previously engaged to a woman and has never before dated a man. Ten years ago, this man would have been portrayed as someone who always knew he was gay but never acknowledged it. But as professor Diamond's research has shown, rather than being set from birth, "change in patterns of same-sex and other-sex attraction is a relatively common experience among sexual minorities."[24]

Diamond clarifies that change is not forged by intentional effort—for example, someone undergoing therapy to try to change their attractions. But change over time and in different circumstances (sometimes called "sexual fluidity") is seen in every category, whether people identify as gay, straight, or bisexual. Diamond recognizes how challenging this finding is to the gay-rights movement:

> We've advocated for the civil rights of LGBT people on the basis of them being LGBT. We have used categories as a part of our strategy for social policy and for acceptance, and that is really, really tricky, now that we know it's not true.[25]

None of this means we choose our attractions, or that everyone who experiences same-sex attraction is also capable of heterosexual desire. But it does mean that sexual orientation is not like race. Our patterns of attraction can change over time. Our racial heritage does not. Out of respect for all concerned, we must untie the knot that has bound these two ideas together.

---

24.   See Lisa M. Diamond, "Sexual Fluidity in Male and Females," *Current Sexual Health Reports* 8 (November 4, 2016): 249–256, https://doi.org/10.1007/s11930-016-0092-z.

25.   Quoted from Diamond, "Just How Different Are Female and Male Sexual Orientation?" See also Clifford J. Rosky and Lisa M. Diamond, "Scrutinizing Immutability: Research on Sexual Orientation and U.S. Legal Advocacy for Sexual Minorities," *The Journal of Sex Research* 53, nos. 4–5 (May–June 2016): 363–91, https://psych.utah.edu/_resources/documents/people/diamond/Scrutinizing%20Immutability.pdf.

But those of us who are Christians must also repent of the ways in which Christian sin has tied that knot.

## RACE, SEXUALITY, AND PREJUDICE

One of the most noxious lies told over centuries about black people was that they were morally inferior to whites. This deep-seated prejudice made 6-year-old Ruby Bridges seem like a threat and made the prosecution lawyer think he knew Anthony Ray Hinton was guilty just by looking at him. King dreamed of a day when his children would be judged not by the color of their skin but by the content of their character, because racial heritage does not carry moral weight. While sexual choices do, we must also recognize that Christians have too often seen people who identify as gay or lesbian through similarly prejudiced eyes.

Many who were raised in the church were taught to be suspicious of gay and lesbian people. In fact, the idea that gay and lesbian people were in some general sense *bad people* was baked into the teaching. When people raised that way discover their prejudices aren't true, they often throw out what the Bible actually says. For example, I've frequently heard straight Christians say something like this: "I used to think that the Bible was against gay marriage, but then I made a gay friend at work. He's really nice and seems to be in a really loving relationship, so now I'm not so sure." When someone says this, it shows that they were raised with views that baptized what the Bible actually says in a steaming pot of prejudice. There's no reason for a Christian to think that someone in a gay relationship is not also kind, generous, and trustworthy. A gay person might well be all these things, just as a straight person who commits adultery might be a nice person in other respects. We might have a gay friend who is faithful to his husband and a straight friend who is not faithful to his wife. If this surprises us, we might need to repent of our prejudice. But we shouldn't repent of our theology.

To be sure, the Bible presents homosexual relationships as a symptom of a generally sinful heart. But this is also true of other forms of sexual sin. People sometimes observe that Christians go easy on straight sin while being strict on gay sin. They're right to cry foul when they see this inconsistency. As we saw in the last chapter, the apostle Paul cried foul too. But the answer is not to say "Yes" to gay marriage because we have so often allowed for sinful heterosexual sex outside marriage. The answer is to say "No" to heterosexual sin as well—which the Bible also condemns.

## WHAT ABOUT PEOPLE WHO ARE ALREADY MARRIED?

An increasingly important question for Christians is what the Bible's teaching means for gay and lesbian people who come to Christ while in a same-sex marriage. The question is particularly pressing for those raising children in same-sex partnerships. The God of the Bible hates divorce. So, isn't it better for those in same-sex marriages to stay married after coming to Christ, just as Paul tells believers who are married to unbelievers not to leave their husband or wife (1 Cor. 7:12–13)?

From a biblical perspective, the answer is No. While same-sex marriage is recognized legally, it is not valid before God, because it requires unrepentant sin. But especially in cases involving children, the church must think creatively about how to welcome new believers into the community of faith. This is one of many areas in which the biblical truth that the church is the primary family unit comes into play. I recently met a woman who is living this reality.

Genia married first at 17 and had her first three children with a chronically unfaithful man. She tried to turn her marriage around, but it didn't work. Instead, she had an affair with another woman, who gave her the relational connection she craved. When her marriage finally broke up, Genia became depressed and suicidal. She was part of a church and had met a young woman named Misha through a friend in her Bible study group. Misha kept vigil over her. "We were at a lake house," Genia recalls. "I could have just walked out into the water."

Misha had no history of same-sex attraction, but one thing led to another and she and Genia fell in love. They moved in together, entered into common-law marriage, and (through a sperm bank) had a child. Everything was well until Misha's grandpa died. She started wondering about mortality and told Genia she wanted to go to church. "I was fine and happy until I went back to church," Genia said. "That was when God started tugging at my heart again." God's call became so clear that Genia told Misha they couldn't go on as they were. At first, Misha took it very badly. But after a period of resisting and even having an affair herself, Misha gave her life to Christ. "Her transformation was amazing," Genia recalls.

All this time, Genia's daughter and son-in-law, who pastors a church in Nashville, had been loving and praying for the two of them. When Genia and Misha came to Christ, they knew they couldn't continue in a sexual relationship. They were open to the possibility that this would mean breaking up their family, and they were ready to take that step—trusting the Lord that their obedience would be best for their daughter as well. But as they prayed, they both felt called instead to restart their lives in the church family Genia's son-in-law served. That church had been deeply instrumental in Misha's faith journey and felt like their spiritual home. So in the end, all three of them moved in with Genia's daughter and son-in-law, who were also raising little girls. Rather than being broken up, their family grew, and their relationship changed. "We were lovers," Genia explains, "and now we're sisters." With words that brought tears to my eyes, Genia told me that she and Misha are closer now as sisters in Christ than they ever were as lovers.

Not every story will have such a happy ending. Some same-sex couples will need full separation to live faithfully for Christ. Painful as this may be, Jesus calls us to deny ourselves and take up our cross and follow him. It isn't safe. But a creative, expansive approach to family will always be part of the answer for gay and lesbian people entering the community of faith: whether they are leaving legal marriages or less formalized relationships, or whether they are simply giving up the possibility of sexual and romantic relationships in the future. Rosaria Butterfield, who was a literature professor at a secular university in a long-term lesbian relationship when she became a Christian, says she learned hospitality from her time in the LGBT+ community.[26] Today, most people associate "non-traditional family"—the sense of corporate closeness that doesn't depend on DNA—with LGBT+ people. But

---

26. Her excellent book, *The Gospel Comes with a House Key: Practicing Radically Ordinary Hospitality in Our Post-Christian World* (Wheaton, IL: Crossway, 2018), makes the case for this being a Christian norm.

the first pioneers of such community were Christians. As one second-century commentator put it, Christians have "a common table, but not a common bed."[27]

## 'WHY HAVE CHRISTIANS ACTED HATEFULLY TOWARD LGBT+ PEOPLE?'

In January 2020, I gave a talk—"Aren't We Better Off Without Christianity?"—for a Christian fellowship at MIT. When it came to Q&A, I asked for questions from skeptical people. One of the first was this: "Why have Christians acted hatefully toward LGBT people?" I said I could answer that important question with one word: sin. Not the sin of the LGBT people who experienced the hate, but the sin of any Christians who deliver it.

Jesus calls us to love even our enemies—let alone those who have made different sexual choices than we have. The ways in which Christians have at times acted hatefully toward gay and lesbian people is simply disobedience to Christ, and its effects can be devastating. The lesbian couple I met with in Missouri were sincerely concerned what I'd say wouldn't be "safe," since some studies have suggested that LGBT+ young adults raised in religious contexts are more likely to attempt suicide than those who weren't. For example, a 2015 study showed that "LGBT young adults who mature in religious contexts have higher odds of suicidal thoughts, and more specifically chronic suicidal thoughts, as well as suicide attempt compared to other LGBT young adults."[28] In general, as we'll see in the next chapter, regular churchgoing has a significant protective effect against suicide. But this does not seem to be the case for those who identify as LGBT+, whose suicide rates in general continue to be much higher than their heterosexual peers, despite greater societal acceptance.[29] Loving a person

---

27.   The Epistle of Mathetes to Diognetus, chapter 5.
28.   See Jeremy J Gibbs and Jeremy Goldbach, "Religious Conflict, Sexual Identity, and Suicidal Behaviors among LGBT Young Adults," *Archives of Suicide Research* 19, no. 4 (March 12, 2015): 472–88, https://pubmed.ncbi.nlm.nih.gov/25763926.
29.   See, for example, Julia Raifman, et al., "Sexual Orientation and Suicide Attempt Disparities Among US Adolescents: 2009–2017," *Pediatrics* 45 no. 3 (March 2020): 1–11, https://pediatrics.

doesn't mean affirming all that person's actions. But it does mean listening and seeking to understand. In *Us versus Them*, Andrew Marin quotes a 29-year-old gay man living in Athens, Georgia, who said something typical of other LGBT+ people he interviewed: "I left the church because I couldn't find one person who cared enough to listen to my story. I mean *really* listen."[30]

If we look at Jesus's life and ministry, we often find him criticized for loving people known for sexual sin. Indeed, he shocked his religious critics when he claimed, "Truly, I say to you, the tax collectors and the prostitutes go into the kingdom of God before you" (Matt. 21:31). Jesus's point was not to affirm prostitution or the extortionate tax collecting of his day. His point was to say, "Look, these people are getting ahead of you, because they realize they're sinners who need me. You guys are sinners too. You just don't realize it!" Some people use this text to argue that Jesus wasn't bothered by sexual sin, so we shouldn't be either. But the opposite is true. In fact, if Jesus had affirmed the sins of the tax collectors and prostitutes, it would have removed what set them apart from the self-righteous Pharisees: they knew they were sinners who needed a Savior.

When Ruby Bridges walked into William Frantz Elementary School, she had to walk past jeering crowds waving hateful signs. Many gay and lesbian people historically have experienced similar treatment in the name of Christianity. Today, such explicit, public hate mainly comes from fringe groups, like the so-called Westboro Baptist Church, which is mostly one man's extended family. But there is still much prejudice in churches, to the extent that it is typically easier to confess to a pornography addiction than to experiencing same-sex attraction, and same-sex attraction is often linked in people's minds with pedophilia. If the beautiful biblical vision of marriage is to shine, this layer of prejudice must be sloughed off.

But while black and LGBT+ experiences have at times been bound together by the unchristian behavior of many professing to follow Christ, we must once again reject a simple narrative of them-and-us.

aappublications.org/content/145/3/e20191658.full.

30.  Andrew Marin, *Us Versus Us: The Untold Story of Religion and the LGBT Community* (Colorado Springs: NavPress, 2016), 35.

Rosaria Butterfield was wooed to Christ by the unconditional love of an older Christian pastor and his wife, whom she met after writing a newspaper article critiquing Christian hate. My friend Rachel was immediately embraced by a Christian fellowship at Yale, and faithful friends walked with her in love and helped her stand again when she fell into sexual sin. And as the 6-year-old Bridges walked past those hateful crowds, she prayed for those who despised her, asking God to forgive them and reflecting true love for enemies. Through centuries of abuse, millions of African American Christians have done the same.

## CAN YOU UNTANGLE THIS FOR ME?

When my daughter came to me with her mess of wool, it was partly an act of confession. Her actions had led to different colors getting tangled up, to knots being pulled more tightly, and to short sections of wool being cut. She had to realize she'd gone wrong and ask for help. If we look back over the last 400 years, we may have a similar realization. It's easy as a Christian today to see the faith of civil-rights leaders such as Martin Luther King Jr. or Fannie Lou Hamer and to feel a warm glow of pride. But that glow turns cold for white Christians like me when we realize that if white Christians had upheld biblical ethics from the first, there would have been no need for the civil-rights movement.

Going further back, I like to think with pride about leading abolitionists like Harriet Tubman or William Wilberforce, whose faith fueled their pursuit of justice. But if white Christians had stood against race-based, chattel slavery in the first place, there would have been no need for the abolitionist movement. Christian sin has allowed the gay-rights movement to trade on the moral capital of the civil-rights movement. "Black lives matter" got tied in people's minds to "love is love" not just because of sin in the world, but because of sin in the church. The sin that protested Ruby Bridges's small steps into an all-white elementary school. The sin that made Richard and Mildred Loving's marriage illegal. The sin that played midwife to the black church, as white believers rejected their brothers and sisters in Christ and refused to worship with them as equals before God. But before we conclude that all this history of Christian sin means we should throw out Christianity, we must remember that human equality is ultimately God-given.

My daughter could have given up her tangled wool entirely and thrown it in the trash. And if we abandon Christianity, we will not find ourselves in a brave new moral world, better able to support equality for all. No, we will find ourselves unable to justify human rights for *anyone*. Without Christianity, human beings have no natural rights, just as chimpanzees, hyenas, and spiders have no rights. And there is no moral arc to the universe. There is nothing but blind, pitiless indifference.

# 4

# "WOMEN'S RIGHTS ARE HUMAN RIGHTS"

In 2019, Margaret Atwood published *The Testaments*, a sequel to her 1985 success *The Handmaid's Tale*. The first book imagined the United States overtaken by a pseudo-Christian sect. In monthly ceremonies, potentially fertile "Handmaids" submit to sex with their assigned "Commanders." Wives supervise. The Handmaids greet each other with a shortened version of Elizabeth's words to the pregnant Mary: "Blessed be the fruit." Atwood's sequel came hot on the heels of a Hulu adaptation that brought *The Handmaid's Tale* to a new generation and made it an icon of resistance against the pro-life movement. Today, protesters wearing the bright red capes and white caps of Atwood's Handmaids visually suggest that any reduction in a woman's right to choose is a religiously motivated threat to women's rights of every kind. Banning abortion would be the ultimate assertion of male control over female bodies. It's a story told in red and white: Christianity is bad for women's rights.

In this chapter, we'll see how wrong that story is. We'll see that without the Bible, there is no basis for women's rights and that Jesus's treatment of women changed their status forever. We'll see that the church has always been disproportionately female, and that rather than benefiting women, the sexual revolution of the 1960s handed us a poisoned chalice. Finally, we'll see that far from being the central plank of women's rights, abortion rots their foundation.

## IN HIS IMAGE

In Genesis 1, God creates humans "male and female" in his image (Gen. 1:27). In the Ancient Near East, this language would have signaled royalty. And in a world in which women were not seen as equal to men, Genesis specifies that female humans bear this godlike stamp. God blesses these first people and tells them to be fruitful and multiply and rule his creation as his deputies (Gen. 1:27–28). To be a woman, first and foremost, is to be made in the image of God.

The equality of men and women is reinforced when the creation of humans is retold in Genesis 2. God makes the man first, but declares it "not good" for him to be alone and plans to make "a helper fit for him" (Gen. 2:18). "Helper" might sound demeaning to us, but in the rest of the Bible, it typically describes God himself, so it cannot signal inferiority.[1] None of the animals is a fitting helper for the man, so God makes woman from man's side. The woman is like the man: *bone of his bones and flesh of his flesh* (Gen. 2:23). She is not an afterthought. She is essential to the project given to humanity in Genesis 1. But the storyline of Genesis 2 makes a point: men and women are created equal and alike, but also meaningfully different from each other—and vitally different from any other animal.

My husband and I are watching *Planet Earth 2*. At times, I've become so invested that I shout, "Run, baby, run!" at little marine iguanas fleeing for their lives from hungry snakes. Most stories include reproduction, whether the month-long courtship dances of high-altitude flamingos or the violent sex of ocean otters. Sometimes females have the upper hand. But sex often asserts male power. For instance, when

---

1. The other use of this exact word is in Ps. 89:19, when the Lord uses it to describe himself helping David. Other examples of the word in different forms include Ex. 18:4; Deut. 33:26, 29; Pss. 20:2; 33:20; 54:4; 118:7; Hos. 13:9. For example, in his final blessings on Israel, Moses says, "There is none like God, O Jeshurun, who rides through the heavens to your help, through the skies in his majesty" (Deut. 33:26). Or the lifeline opening of Ps. 121: "I lift up my eyes to the hills. From where does my help come? My help comes from the Lord, who made heaven and earth" (vv. 1–2).

introducing us to a female snow leopard and her 2-year-old daughter, the narrator warned that male snow leopards often kill cubs not their own. This mother managed to distract the male enough for the cub to escape, but she was injured during his sexual assault. Watching this series is a stark reminder: as close as we may be to our pets, and as much as we may identify with baby iguanas, if we are going to lay claim to women's rights, we need a reason why we are not *just* animals.

To be clear, I have no problem identifying as a mammal. Female mammals are warm-blooded, have hair, give birth, and nourish their young with milk. I check every box! My faith gives me no reason to say I'm *not* an animal. But it gives me *every* reason to say I'm not *just* an animal—not because my body doesn't fit the bill, but because my Creator says so. Humans alone are made in the image of God.

Many secular people see evolution as an origin story that replaces the Genesis account. The theory of evolution doesn't by itself disprove God's creation or show that we're not set apart by him. Some of the top evolutionary scientists in the world, in fact, are serious Christians.[2] But if evolution is our *only* origin story, then Yuval Noah Harari's earlier observation is right: we humans have no natural rights, just as chimpanzees, hyenas, and spiders have no natural rights. We only have the triumph of the strong over the weak. As men are almost always physically stronger than women, we have no grounds for saying women are equal to men. And if our only purpose is to propagate our DNA, we have no grounds for saying rape is wrong. Feminists rightly object to women being treated like wombs on legs, valued only for our reproductive power. But if evolution is our only origin story, that is precisely what we women are.

So why do so many secular people believe in gender equality?

## HOW THE CHRISTIAN REVOLUTION REMADE THE WORLD

Historian Tom Holland stopped believing in the Bible as a boy. He was far more attracted to Greek and Roman gods than to the crucified hero of the Christian faith. But after years of research, Holland has concluded that even secular Westerners are deeply shaped by Chris-

2. See *Confronting Christianity*, chapter 6 for a fuller exploration.

tianity. In particular, he argues, people on all sides of today's debates about gender and sexuality depend on Christian ideas:

> That every human being possessed an equal dignity was not remotely a self-evident truth. A Roman would have laughed at it. To campaign against discrimination on the grounds of gender or sexuality, however, was to depend on large numbers of people sharing in a common assumption: that everyone possessed an inherent worth. The origins of this principle . . . lay not in the French Revolution, nor in the Declaration of Independence, nor in the Enlightenment, but in the Bible.[3]

In Greco-Roman thinking, men were superior to women and sex was a way to prove it. "As captured cities were to the swords of the legions," Holland explains, "so the bodies of those used sexually were to the Roman man. To be penetrated, male or female, was to be branded as inferior."[4] In Rome, "men no more hesitated to use slaves and prostitutes to relieve themselves of their sexual needs than they did to use the side of a road as a toilet."[5] The idea that every woman had the right to choose what happened to her body would've been laughable.

Christianity threw out this model. Rather than being seen as inferior to men, women were equally made in God's image. Rather than being free to use slaves and prostitutes (of either sex), men were expected to be faithful to one wife, or to live in celibate singleness. Ironically, the scenario described in *The Handmaid's Tale*—a man sleeping with an enslaved woman—is one of the exact things Christianity outlawed. The Christian husband was to love his wife as Christ loved the church (Eph. 5:25). The relative weakness of her body was not a license for domination, but a reason to show her honor as a fellow heir of the grace of life (1 Pet. 3:7). While Roman families often married off their prepubescent daughters, Christian women could marry later. A woman whose husband had died was affirmed in remaining single, but also free to marry any man she wished, so long as he belonged to the Lord (1 Cor. 7:39–40).

3.    Holland, *Dominion*, 494.
4.    Holland, *Dominion*, 99.
5.    Holland, *Dominion*, 99.

No wonder Christianity was so attractive to women. Jesus had changed everything.

## JESUS'S SHOCKING RELATIONSHIPS WITH WOMEN

If we could read the Gospels through first-century eyes, Jesus's treatment of women would knock us to our knees. We saw in chapter 1 that his longest recorded conversation with any individual was with a Samaritan woman of ill repute (John 4:7–30). But this wasn't an isolated incident. Jesus repeatedly welcomed women his contemporaries despised. One time, he was dining at a Pharisee's house when a "sinful woman" gatecrashed. She wept on Jesus's feet, wiped them with her hair, and kissed them. The Pharisee was appalled: "If this man were a prophet, he would have known who and what sort of woman this is who is touching him, for she is a sinner" (Luke 7:39). But Jesus turned the tables on his host and affirmed this woman as an example of love (Luke 7:36–50). He welcomed women despised as sexual sinners. He also welcomed women deemed unclean.

One day, Jesus was on his way to heal a 12-year-old girl when a woman who had suffered 12 years of menstrual bleeding figured that if she could just touch the fringe of his clothes she'd be made well. She was right. But Jesus didn't just move on. He had her come forward from the crowd and commended her faith (Luke 8:43–48). When Jesus finally reached the sick 12-year-old, she was dead. But it wasn't too late. Speaking Aramaic, their shared mother tongue, Jesus said, "Little girl, I say to you, arise," and she got up (Mark 5:41). Whether little girls or prostitutes, whether despised foreigners or women made unclean by menstrual blood, whether married or single, sick (Matt. 8:14–16) or disabled (Luke 13:10–16), Jesus made time for women and treated them with care and respect. In Luke's Gospel, women are often compared with men, and where there is a contrast, the women come out looking better.[6] In all four Gospels, women witness Jesus's resurrection first—although the testimony of women wouldn't have been seen as convincing at that time.

6.   See discussion in *Confronting Christianity*, 126–28.

We gain an intimate glimpse of Jesus's relationships with women in his friendship with two sisters. We first meet Mary and Martha in Luke, when Jesus is at their house. Martha is busy serving. Mary is sitting at Jesus's feet, learning with the disciples. Martha complains and asks Jesus to tell Mary she should be serving, too. But Jesus responds: "Mary has chosen the good portion, which will not be taken away from her" (Luke 10:42). In a culture in which women were expected to serve, not to learn, Jesus affirms Mary's learning from him. But far from dismissing Martha, John tells another story in which Jesus has a stunning conversation with her after her brother Lazarus has died. In fact, it seems that Jesus let Lazarus die partly so that he could have this conversation with Martha—whom he loved (John 1:5)—in which he uttered world-changing words: "I am the resurrection and the life. Whoever believes in me, though he die, yet shall he live, and everyone who lives and believes in me shall never die. Do you believe this?" (John 11:25–26).

Martha did. So have countless women since.

## DISPROPORTIONATELY FEMALE CHURCH

In the early second century, Roman governor Pliny the Younger wrote to the emperor Trajan for advice on how to deal with Christians. The "contagion" of Christianity was spreading: "many persons of every age, every rank, and also of both sexes" were at risk. To find out more about Christianity, Pliny had tortured "two female slaves who were called deaconesses."[7] From other accounts of early Christianity, these female slaves seem representative. In fact, it seems that there were roughly twice as many women in the early church as men, many of them slaves.[8] One second-century Greek philosopher quipped that Christians "want and are able to convince only the foolish, dishonorable and stupid, only slaves, women, and little children." Likewise, in the third century, Christianity was mocked for attracting "the dregs

7.  See Michael J. Kruger, *Christianity at the Crossroads: How the Second Century Shaped the Future of the Church* (Downers Grove, IL: IVP Academic, 2018), 32.
8.  See Rodney Stark, *The Rise of Christianity: How the Obscure, Marginal Jesus Movement Became the Dominant Religious Force in the Western World in a Few Centuries* (Princeton, NJ: Princeton University Press, 1996), 97–110.

of the populace and credulous women with the inability natural to their sex."[9]

That the early church was as much as two-thirds female is especially surprising given that the Greco-Roman empire was disproportionately male. Many women died in childbirth, and many baby girls were abandoned: distressing proof that women were seen as less precious than men. But given the way Jesus treated women, it's no surprise that women flocked to him. And they're flocking still.

Women tend to be more religious than men are, but the effect is most pronounced with Christianity. Globally, women are more likely to identify as Christians, and Christian women are more likely to attend church and pray.[10] This gender imbalance holds in the United States, where women are more likely to say they pray daily (64 percent vs. 47 percent) and attend religious services weekly (40 percent vs. 32 percent).[11] But the gender gap is even greater in the country soon to become home to the largest number of Christians in the world. Much of the church in China is underground, so data is hard to collect. But there's evidence to suggest that the Chinese church is also at least two thirds female, despite the general population being disproportionately male.[12]

So why are modern women in countries as different as the United States and China choosing Christianity? Haven't men used Christianity to denigrate and control women? Isn't Christianity against women's rights, from sexual freedoms to equality in the workplace? Doesn't Christianity subjugate women, in the home and in the church? As we'll see in the rest of this chapter, it's not so simple.

9.   See Kruger, *Christianity at the Crossroads*, 34–35.

10.  In a 2016 survey of 192 countries, for example, 33.7 percent of women identified as Christian versus 29.9 percent of men. See "The Gender Gap in Religion Around the World," Pew Research Center, March 22, 2016, https://www.pewresearch.org/wp-content/uploads/sites/7/2016/03/Religion-and-Gender-Full-Report.pdf.

11.  "The Gender Gap in Religion Around the World," Pew Forum, March 22, 2016, https://www.pewforum.org/2016/03/22/the-gender-gap-in-religion-around-the-world.

12.  For example, a 2007 survey found that 73.2 percent of Chinese Protestants surveyed were women. See F. Yang et al. "Spiritual Life Study of Chinese Residents," *Association of Religion Data Archives*, September 16, 2019, https://www.thearda.com/Archive/Files/Descriptions/SPRTCHNA.asp. Likewise, members of house churches in China are estimated to be 80 percent female. See David Aikman, *Jesus in Beijing: How Christianity is Transforming China and Changing the Global Balance of Power* (Washington, DC: Regnery, 2003), 98.

## CHRISTIANITY AND FEMINISM

Like many movement-making words, *feminism* is a charged and changing term. Many today insist it includes things Christians can't affirm—in particular, abortion. But the definition of feminism is:

1. The theory of the political, economic, and social equality of the sexes.
2. Organized activity on behalf of women's rights and interests.[13]

There are many things that have been fought for under the banner of feminism that Christians can and should affirm: for example, women's right to vote, hold property, and be paid the same as a man for doing the same job. Indeed, many early feminists advocated for women's rights *because* they were Christians. For these reasons, I'm happy to call myself a feminist, even if I have to explain what I do and don't mean. I believe that women are equal to men. I believe we should have many opportunities that have historically been denied to us, and that we should be paid the same salary for the same work. But rather than see abortion rights as the central plank of the feminist structure, I believe its central plank should be the cross.

As we've seen, the biblical creation stories and the life and teachings of Jesus present men and women as equally precious in God's eyes. Many think this edifice was undermined when Paul called wives to submit to their husbands. But as we saw in chapter 2, far from asserting male superiority, Paul calls husbands to sacrifice for their wives, giving themselves up like Christ on the cross. If we make husbands and wives interchangeable, we lose the gospel message that marriage is designed to preach, and we do violence to the word of life to which women have been drawn for millennia. Of course, we must recognize that men throughout the centuries have often failed to live up to this vision and have used texts like Ephesians 5 to subjugate and denigrate women. Some continue to do this today. But just as the failure of white Christians to love and respect their black brothers

13. See "Feminism," Merriam-Webster Dictionary, https://www.merriam-webster.com/dictionary/feminism.

and sisters arose not from too much obedience to the Bible but too little, so the failure of Christian husbands to love and serve their wives comes from ignoring what the Bible really says.

We find a similar problem when we see Paul assigning some leadership roles in the church to qualified men and assume this asserts male superiority. When the mother of Jesus's disciples James and John asked for special leadership roles for her sons in his kingdom, Jesus replied, "You do not know what you are asking" (Matt. 20:22). This mother thought she was securing status for her sons. But Jesus said she was securing suffering. He asked James and John if they were able to drink the cup he was going to drink, referring to his horrifying death. When the other disciples were angry with these brothers, Jesus explained they were all getting it wrong. In the world, leadership meant self-serving power. But in Jesus's kingdom, being great meant becoming a slave, "just as the Son of Man did not come to be served, but to serve, and to give his life as a ransom for many" (Matt. 20:26–28).

If we listen to Jesus, leadership in the church isn't about power and privilege. It's about service and sacrifice. We easily forget this in a world of Western comforts. But in the early church and in much of the global church today, leading a church means risking your life. God made men physically stronger than women and then put them in the firing line. In a world in which strength meant dominance, Jesus got down on his knees and washed his disciples' feet, before being lifted up on a cross. Where the Bible gives different roles to men and women, it calls men first to come and die.

What's more, while Paul seems to give certain specific roles in the church to men, he also explicitly values the ministry of women. For example, he tells the Christians in Rome to welcome the woman delivering his letter:

> I commend to you our sister Phoebe, a servant of the church at
> Cenchreae, that you may welcome her in the Lord in a way worthy of

the saints, and help her in whatever she may need from you, for she has
been a patron of many and of myself as well. (Rom. 16:1–2)

Paul greets a married couple, Prisca and Aquilla, whom he calls "my
fellow workers in Christ Jesus, who risked their necks for my life" (vv.
3–4), and he greets seven other women, including "Mary, who has
worked hard for you" (v. 6) and Tryphena and Tryphosa, whom he
calls "workers in the Lord" (v. 12).

While the Bible clearly values the work of raising children that
women often undertake, it also greatly values women's gospel ministry
outside the home, and gives us positive examples of women working
for pay. The ideal wife described in Proverbs 31 makes money from
her work outside the home, and some of the first female Christians
held paid jobs. For example, Lydia—one of the first people to follow
Christ in Philippi—was a "seller of purple goods" (Acts 16:14). She
opened her home to the apostles, and it seems likely that the Philip-
pian church continued to meet at her house. At no point was Lydia
rebuked for having a job, and nothing in the Bible suggests that wom-
en should be paid less than men for the same work.

Some of my female Christian friends are married. Some are single.
Some are in secular work. Some work for Christian ministries. Some
work full time, some work part time, and some are full time with
their children. I'm grateful for the opportunities they have to serve the
Lord in each of these situations. Many of these freedoms have been
argued for by feminists. But many Christians understandably don't
want to identify as feminists—despite believing that men and wom-
en are equal—because some of the beliefs associated with feminism
today can't be endorsed by Christians. Before coming to the central
plank of abortion, we must see the larger structure it upholds: a structure built by the so-called sexual revolution.

## FALLOUT OF THE SEXUAL REVOLUTION

The sexual revolution of the 1960s was sold to us as the liberation of
women. For centuries, men had been finding ways to sneak around
marriage and have commitment-free sex. Thanks to the pill, now
women could as well. But in the last 60 years, despite gains in free-

dom and opportunities, women's self-reported happiness in America has declined.[14] Why? Part of the reason is that commitment-free sex is a poisoned chalice.

Stable marriage correlates with mental and physical health benefits for both men and women. But being married seems to be a particularly significant factor in happiness for women.[15] Conversely, multiple studies have shown that for women in particular, increasing our number of sexual partners correlates with worse mental health, including higher levels of sadness, suicidal ideation, depression, and drug abuse.[16] This isn't because women are uninterested in sex. But married people experience more and better sex than their unmarried peers do.[17] In fact, a recent study found that women in *highly* religious marriages (couples who pray together, read Scripture at home, attend church, and so on) were twice as likely as their secular peers to say they were satisfied with their sexual relationship.[18]

Christian marriage has long been seen by secular liberals as a repressive institution designed to hold women down. But in 2016, a study of women in America found that highly religious women married to highly religious men who agreed with the statement, "It is usually better for everyone involved if the father takes the lead in

14. See, for example, Betsey Stevenson and Justin Wolfers, "The Paradox of Declining Female Happiness," IZA Discussion Paper, May 2009, http://ftp.iza.org/dp4200.pdf, and Jason L. Cummings, "Assessing U.S. Racial and Gender Differences in Happiness, 1972–2016: An Intersectional Approach," *Journal of Happiness Studies* 21 (2020): 709–32, https://doi.org/10.1007/s10902-019-00103-z.

15. See, for example, "Subjective Health and Happiness in the United States: Gender Differences in the Effects of Socioeconomic Status Indicators," *Journal of Mental Health and Clinical Psychology* 4, no. 2 (May 14, 2020): 8–17, https://www.ncbi.nlm.nih.gov/pmc/articles/PMC7304555.

16. See, for example, Tyree Oredein and Cristine Delnevo, "The Relationship between Multiple Sexual Partners and Mental Health in Adolescent Females," Community Medicine and Health Education, December 23, 2013, https://www.omicsonline.org/the-relationship-between-multiple-sexual-partners-and-mental-health-in-adolescent-females-2161-0711.1000256.php?aid=21466; and Sandhya Ramrakha et al., "The Relationship between Multiple Sex Partners and Anxiety, Depression, and Substance Dependence Disorders: A Cohort Study," NCBI, February 12, 2013, https://www.ncbi.nlm.nih.gov/pmc/articles/PMC3752789.

17. See, for example, Stephen Cranney, "The Influence of Religiosity/Spirituality on Sex Life Satisfaction and Sexual Frequency: Insights from the Baylor Religion Survey," *Review of Religious Research* 62 (January 1, 2020): 289–314, https://doi.org/10.1007/s13644-019-00395-w.

18. Matthew Saxey and Hal Boyd, "Do 'Church Ladies' Really Have Better Sex Lives?," Institute for Family Studies, November 16, 2020, https://ifstudies.org/blog/do-church-ladies-really-have-better-sex-lives.

working outside the home and the mother takes the lead in caring for the home and family" are the happiest wives: 73 percent say the relationship quality of their marriage is above average. The next happiest were religious women married to religious men who disagreed with that statement—60 percent reported above-average satisfaction. Both groups were happier than women in secular marriages.[19] Ironically, the demographic most pitied by secular progressives—women in religious marriages—are happier than those who pity them. But the reason isn't just that they're happily married. Being actively religious gives women a boost in happiness. In fact, it can be lifesaving.

## DEATHS OF DESPAIR

In October 2019, I wrote to Tyler VanderWeele—a professor at the Harvard School of Public Health—because I was shocked. I knew from his research that weekly church attendance was associated with better mental health and lower rates of suicide. But I didn't know how big the difference was. I'd just read a paper on one large-scale study of U.S. women that found those who attended religious services at least once a week were *five times less likely to kill themselves* than those who never attended.[20] I was so stunned I wrote to Tyler to check that this was a representative result. He answered, "Yes! Studies suggest three- to six-fold lower rates. It may be one of the most protective factors known for suicide!"

In May 2020, Tyler's team published a new, large-scale study with similarly striking results. After controlling for multiple relevant factors, it found that women who attend religious services weekly were 68 percent less likely to die "deaths of despair" (deaths due to suicide, drug overdose, or alcohol) than those who never attended. Men who

19.    See W. Bradford Wilcox, Jason S. Carroll, and Laurie DeRose, "Religious Men Can Be Devoted Dads, Too," *The New York Times*, May 18, 2019, https://www.nytimes.com/2019/05/18/opinion/sunday/happy-marriages.html.

20.    See Tyler J. VanderWeele et al., "Association Between Religious Service Attendance and Lower Suicide Rates Among US Women," *JAMA Psychology*, August 2016, https://jamanetwork.com/journals/jamapsychiatry/article-abstract/2529152.

attended weekly were 33 percent less likely to die such deaths.[21] The effect of religious participation is remarkable. But going to church seems to have the strongest effect on women. The results aren't unique to Christianity, though most of the U.S. data is from churchgoers.

It seems that, for an alarming number of women, rejecting religion isn't a passport to life but a ticket to despair. The lesbian couple I mentioned in chapter 2, who asked whether what I was going to say about gender and sexuality would be safe, are raising two daughters. Loving parents though they clearly are, they're raising their girls with one of the practices most associated with suicide: *not* going to church.

But if secularization and the sexual revolution didn't lead to greater happiness for women, are we at least doing good to women by allowing them to choose abortion?

## BRIEF HISTORY OF INFANTICIDE

One of the brute facts by which we can judge how the ancient world valued women is the common practice of abandoning baby girls. As we saw earlier, the practice of leaving newborn girls to die led to a gender imbalance in the Greco-Roman empire. We gain a sobering insight into this from a letter by a Roman soldier to his wife in 1 BC. The otherwise affectionate letter includes this instruction: "Above all, if you bear a child and it is male, let it be; if it is female, cast it out."[22] Babies with disabilities were also discarded. In fact, the Greek philosopher Aristotle had pitched for eugenics legislation: "Let there be a law that no deformed child shall live."[23]

The idea of abandoning baby girls is alien to us. But even today, we see this practice continuing in the two largest countries that haven't yet been significantly shaped by Christianity. The Chinese church is growing so fast that it could reshape Chinese culture in the next generation. But selective abortion and infanticide in past generations

21. See Ying Chen, et al., "Religious Service Attendance and Deaths Related to Drugs, Alcohol, and Suicide Among US Health Care Professionals," *JAMA Psychiatry* 77, no. 7 (May 6, 2020): 737–44, https://jamanetwork.com/journals/jamapsychiatry/article-abstract/2765488.

22. *Letter of Hilarion*, P.Oxy. 4 744, http://www.papyri.info/apis/toronto.apis.17.

23. Aristotle, *Politics*, 7.14.10. Aristotle, *The Politics*, ed. Stephen Everson (Cambridge: Cambridge University Press, 1988), 192.

have led to a gender gap of 35 million. Likewise in India, where Hinduism is the dominant religion, the gender gap from selective abortion and infanticide is 25 million.[24] So what has changed our ideas about the abandonment of newborns in general and of newborn girls in particular? Jesus.

Jesus's valuing of babies is as striking as his valuing of women. Right after Jesus preached against divorce (a practice that left women and children abandoned), people tried to bring their little children to him for his blessing (Matt. 19:3–15; Mark 10:2–16). Luke says they were bringing "even infants" (Luke 18:15). Jesus's disciples turned them away. But Jesus rebuked them:

> Let the children come to me; do not hinder them, for to such belongs the kingdom of God. Truly, I say to you, whoever does not receive the kingdom of God like a child shall not enter it. (Mark 10:14–15)

Then Jesus took the children and babies in his arms and blessed them. We do not feel the shock of his words and actions. But his first hearers did.

Paul Offit, a non-Christian professor of pediatrics at University of Pennsylvania, calls Christianity "the single greatest breakthrough against child abuse" in history. He explains:

> At the time of Jesus' life . . . child abuse, as noted by one historian, was "the crying vice of the Roman Empire." Infanticide was common. Abandonment was common . . . children were property, no different than slaves. But Jesus stood up for children, cared about them, when those around him typically didn't.[25]

Taking their cues from Jesus, the early Christians collected the babies abandoned by others. And when (to everyone's surprise) the Roman

---

24. Elaine Storkey, "Violence against Women Begins in the Womb," *Christianity Today*, May 2, 2018  https://www.christianitytoday.com/women/2018/may/violence-againstwomen-begins-in-womb-abortion.html.

25. Paul A. Offit, "Why I Wrote This Book: Paul A. Offit, M.D., Bad Faith: When Religious Belief Undermines Modern Medicine," Hamilton and Griffin on Rights, March 17, 2015, https://

emperor Constantine became a Christian, legal protections for women and children started to come into place.

In the early fourth century, Constantine passed laws protecting women from unwarranted divorce and offering provision for children born into poverty: "If any parent should report that he has offspring which on account of poverty he is not able to rear, there shall be no delay in issuing food and clothing."[26] Historian John Dickson notes that Constantine used churches "as the welfare distribution centres for this program."[27] Killing an infant became a form of homicide in AD 374, under a subsequent Christian emperor. In our culture, pro-lifers are often accused of not caring about vulnerable mothers and children *after* birth. But the first Christ-motivated pro-life legislation in the world followed laws protecting women from abandonment and providing for poor families. Consistent Christian ethics must do all these things. It's no coincidence that in Matthew and Mark, Jesus's teaching on marriage and welcoming children is followed by his instruction to the rich young man to sell all he has and give it to the poor.

Today, as in the first century, two symbiotic factors put babies at risk: poverty and fatherlessness. In the United States in 2018, 85 percent of women seeking abortions were unmarried and about three quarters were living below or not far above the federal poverty line. Due largely to historic inequalities, this means that black babies are more than three times as likely to be aborted as white babies.[28] These tiny black lives matter. But rather than providing women with the

casetext.com/analysis/why-i-wrote-this-book-paul-a-offit-md-bad-faith-when-religious-belief-undermines-modern-medicine.

26. *Theodosian Code* 11.27.1–2.

27. See John Dickson, *Bullies and Saints: An Honest Look at the Good and Evil of Christian History* (Zondervan: Grand Rapids, 2021), 76. See pp. 33–36 and 74–76 for a broader discussion.

28. See Katherine Kortsmit, Tara C. Jatlaoui, Michele G. Mandel, Jennifer A. Reeves, Titilope Oduyebo, Emily Petersen, and Maura K. Whiteman, "Abortion Surveillance — United States, 2018," *Morbidity and Mortality Weekly Report* 69, no. 7 (Summer 2020), http://dx.doi.org/10.15585/mmwr.ss6907a1; and Tara C. Jatlaoui, Lindsay Eckhaus, Michele G. Mandel, Antoinette Nguyen, Titilope Oduyebo, Emily Petersen, and Maura K. Whiteman, "Abortion Surveillance — United States, 2016," *Morbidity and Mortality Weekly Report Surveillance Summaries* 68, no. 11 (November 29, 2019): 1–41, http://dx.doi.org/10.15585/mmwr.ss6811a1. See also Jenna Jerman, Rachel K. Jones, and Tsuyoshi Onda, "Characteristics of U.S. Abortion Patients in 2014 and Changes Since 2008," *Guttmacher Institute Report*, May 2016, https://www.guttmacher.org/report/characteristics-us-abortion-patients-2014.

support they need, our society opts for the quick fix of abortion. Thankfully, abortion rates in America are trending down—2018 saw the lowest rate on record. But that still represents 619,591 lost lives.

What's more, far from being a public good, abortion pushes an alarmingly low fertility rate down yet further. With a fertility rate at 1.78 babies per woman—significantly below the replacement rate of 2.1—the United States is sitting on the demographic time bomb of an aging society. To be clear, the value of life should never be measured in economic terms. But contrary to the prevailing myth that children are a burden on society, from a purely economic perspective, we need more kids. Most women also want more children. In America, "the gap between the number of children that women say they want to have (2.7) and the number of children they will probably actually have (1.8) has risen to the highest level in 40 years."[29] And contrary to popular imagination, the vast majority of abortions do not arise from teenage pregnancies, but are sought by women who—with the right support—could be in a good position to raise these children.[30]

The Bible doesn't call us to a pseudo-Christian past, when the West was supposedly controlled by Christian norms, but men were all too often excused to sleep with prostitutes and servant girls and pregnant women were abandoned by the thousands. It doesn't call us to a world in which unmarried mothers are despised or marginalized and forced into back-street abortions. Rather, God calls us to a world in which women are seen as equal to men, regardless of their marital status; in which pregnant women are supported; in which men are called either to be faithful husbands or faithful singles; and in which babies are valued and provided for—not just by their biological parents, but by their spiritual family writ large. To solve the problem of abortion, we don't need one law reversed. We need a loving revolution.

But is abortion actually a moral problem? Isn't it quite different from infanticide, which we'd all agree is unacceptable?

29. Lyman Stone, "American Women Are Having Fewer Children Than They'd Like," *The New York Times*, February 13, 2018, https://www.nytimes.com/2018/02/13/upshot/american-fertility-is-falling-short-of-what-women-want.html.

30. In 2018, adolescents aged <15 and 15–19 years accounted for 0.2 percent and 8.8 percent of all reported abortions. See "Abortion Surveillance — United States, 2018."

# IS ABORTION DIFFERENT FROM INFANTICIDE?

When I first engaged these debates as a teenager, most pro-choice advocates argued for a bright white line between abortion and infanticide. Pro-life folk insisted that there is no line. Sure, we could set a point at which we suddenly declared an unborn human. But whatever point we picked—for example, the time from which the infant would likely survive outside the womb—was arbitrary. As medical technology advanced, the age of viability changed. But babies didn't. To consider babies at 22 weeks gestation to be human today, when 10 years ago they would not have been, made little sense.

My niece, who is now 16, was delivered at 24 weeks and 5 days. Her newborn body was so small that her father's wedding ring could fit around her upper arm. At the time, she was on the edge of viability. In many other countries, she certainly would've died. After birth, she enjoyed every legal protection and medical support. But the day before delivery, her mother could legally have chosen to abort: she had preeclampsia, and her life was under threat. In many states, she could've been aborted a week earlier without this threat. At that age, was my niece a human being? Undoubtedly. Did she have human rights? It depends whom you ask.

Today, rather than denying that unborn babies are human beings, pro-choice advocates tend to distinguish between a human *being* and a human *person*. We're all human beings by virtue of our species. But to be a human *person*—someone with human rights—we must have certain capacities. The problem is, when people start identifying those capacities, they realize newborn infants don't have them either. In 2012, medical ethicists Alberto Giubilini and Francesca Minerva published a paper in the *Journal of Medical Ethics* arguing that "both fetuses and newborns do not have the same moral status as actual persons," so "after-birth abortion (killing a newborn) should be permissible in all the cases where abortion is, including cases where the newborn is not disabled."[31] Most pro-choice activists wouldn't go this far. The question is: Why not?

31.   Alberto Giubilini and Francesca Minerva, "After-Birth Abortion: Why Should the Baby Live?," *Journal of Medical Ethics* 39, no. 5 (May 2013): 1, https://pubmed.ncbi.nlm.nih.

One of the leading philosophers to argue for the being-person distinction is Princeton professor Peter Singer. He faces the fact that atheism doesn't justify a distinction between humans and other animals. So, rather than anchoring value in our being human, he argues that beings (human or otherwise) should be valued according to their capacities. In Singer's view, "A week-old baby is not a rational and self-conscious being, and there are many nonhuman animals whose rationality, self-consciousness, awareness, capacity, and so on, exceed that of a human baby a week or a month old." Therefore, Singer concludes, "The life of a newborn baby is of less value . . . than the life of a pig, a dog, or a chimpanzee."[32] To translate this into practical terms, eating bacon might be more immoral than infanticide.

This logic shocked one of the few people who knew both me and my husband before we knew each other.

## UNEXPECTED CONVERT

I met Sarah Irving-Stonebraker when we were both graduate students at Cambridge. She was a convinced atheist and believed that abortion is a woman's right. After finishing her PhD she won a postdoctoral fellowship at Oxford, where she attended a series of lectures by Peter Singer. Sarah had been raised by loving, non-religious parents, who taught her to believe in human rights. But as she heard this famous atheist philosopher explain that simply being human doesn't mean you should have human rights—and that infanticide is morally justifiable—she began to realize that her atheism stuck a knife in the back of her deepest moral beliefs. As a secular liberal, Sarah had thought Christianity was the enemy of human rights, care for the poor, racial justice, and equality for women. But she gradually discovered it was the basis for those things. Eventually, as assistant professor of history at Florida State University at age 28, she turned to Jesus.

In becoming a Christian, Sarah has changed her mind about many things, including abortion. But she doesn't believe in the equality of men and women less since she converted. In fact, she believes in it

gov/22361296.

32.   Peter Singer, *Practical Ethics*, 2nd ed. (Cambridge: Cambridge University Press, 1999), 169.

more. Now, instead of "just a well-meaning conceit of liberalism," her belief in universal human value is grounded in God's creation of all humans in his image and in the overwhelming love of God in Christ that is "utterly unlike anything which [she] had expected, or of which [she] could make sense." Christianity, Sarah realized, is ultimately "far more radical than the leftist ideologies with which [she] had previously been enamored."[33] Jesus's death on the cross for us upended all our human views of power and made the weak as precious as the strong.

But what about women left in desperate circumstances? What about cases of rape or risk to the mother's life? What about the women who just don't want to have the child they have conceived? Shouldn't women ultimately have the right to choose?

## SHOULD WOMEN HAVE THE RIGHT TO CHOOSE?

One powerful claim of the pro-choice movement is that women should have the right to decide what they do with their bodies. In most situations, I strongly agree. As we saw earlier, one of the stark contrasts between Christianity and the Greco-Roman world was the idea that women's bodies *weren't* just objects to be used by men. The sex slavery of *The Handmaid's Tale* is utterly at odds with Christianity.

Christians absolutely believe that a woman should have the right to choose not to have sex. What's more, we believe a woman shouldn't be pressured into sex, as all too many women are today. (One friend who had moved from Manhattan to Boston told me that in Manhattan you were expected to sleep with a guy on the second date, while in Boston you might reach the third before he pushed for sex.) But whatever our perspectives on abortion, none of us believes a woman should have the right to choose what she does with her body in every respect. As a woman, I have the right to choose not to have sex with you. But unless you're assaulting me or someone else, I don't have the right to punch you in the face. Both sex and punching are things I do with my body. But one would hurt *your* body, and your body matters too.

---

33. See Sarah Irving-Stonebraker, "How Oxford and Peter Singer Drove Me from Atheism to Jesus," The Veritas Forum, May 22, 2017, http://www.veritas.org/oxford-atheism-to-jesus.

What if the scenario wasn't so simple? What if you'd slipped over the edge of a cliff, and the only thing keeping you from falling to your death was me holding your hand? What if my arm was in serious pain, and my shoulder was dislocated by your weight? What if I'd been forced by someone else to hold your hand before you slipped? Would I have the right to choose to let go? No. I'd need to hold on as long as possible, until some other help could come. My body matters. But your body matters too.

My niece was born prematurely because her mother had pre-eclampsia. To carry her baby to term would've killed my sister-in-law, but she carried my niece for as long as possible with the hope she'd survive. Both their lives mattered, and thank God, both survived. I have no wish to oversimplify. There will be times when tragedy is inevitable and terrible choices must be made. But if Christianity is true, then both mother and baby matter. And if there is no God, then ultimately neither do.

If there is no God who made us in his image—if, as Harari puts it, "human rights are . . . figments of our fertile imaginations"—then a baby in her mother's womb *is* just a collection of cells.[34] But if there is no God who made us in his image, then that's what you and I are too. Pregnant women have no natural rights, just as chimpanzees, hyenas, and spiders have no rights. If we're no more than animals, the statement "Women's Rights Are Human Rights" isn't worth the yard sign on which it is written.

But if Christianity is true, the central plank of women's rights isn't our right to have our unborn babies killed. The central plank of women's rights is Mary's unborn child, who grew to be the man who valued us so much he died on a Roman cross so we could live. Filled with the Holy Spirit, Elizabeth shouted to her pregnant cousin Mary, "Blessed are you among women, and blessed is the fruit of your womb!" (Luke 1:41–42). *The Handmaid's Tale* contorts these words into a modern curse. But truly this baby conceived out of wedlock and born into poverty changed everything for women. Blessed be the fruit.

34. Harari, *Sapiens*, 32

# 5

# "TRANSGENDER WOMEN ARE WOMEN"

At the beginning of the film *Mulan* (2020), we see a young girl with extraordinary gifts. Mulan wields a stick like a swordsman, scales walls, and runs on roofs. "Your chi is strong," her father declares. "But chi is for warriors, not daughters." Mulan's role is to marry well. But her meeting with the matchmaker is disastrous, and when imperial messengers come to conscript one man from every family, she steals her father's armor and sword and runs away to train for war. "We're going to make men out of every single one of you," her new commander boasts.

Mulan didn't fit her role at home. But when the soldiers pledge to be "loyal, brave, and true," she cannot echo the last word. The only person who sees through Mulan's disguise is her nemesis Xianniang—another warrior woman who was rejected by her community because her chi was "beyond imagining." Xianniang goads Mulan to speak the truth. When she refuses, Xianniang shoots to kill. Mulan is saved by the leather that binds her breasts. She gets up, throws off her armor, and returns to the battle as the chi-filled woman she is. When she finally comes home, her father greets her with these moving words: "One warrior knows another. You were always there. Yet I see you for the first time."

The questions in this chapter cut deep into identity. What is the truth of you and me? Is there something other than our bodies that defines our male or femaleness: something like chi, perhaps, that belongs to men but might also make a warrior woman? Is sex binary or a spectrum? How can people who don't feel like they fit with their biological sex be seen and known for who they truly are? And what does the Bible have to say about all this?

While not yet etched on our neighborhood signs, "Transgender Women Are Women" is edging into the secular creed. In this chapter, we'll see that if this claim is true, then "woman" has no meaning anymore. We'll notice the long history of a small number of males experiencing alienation from their sex that starts in childhood and may or may not resolve by adulthood, and a recent upsurge of adolescent girls identifying as transgender, often without any known history of gender dysphoria. We'll see that some people are born with intersex conditions, but that this does not mean we should abandon the reality of male-female sex difference. We'll recognize that whereas transgender-identifying people may not be more vulnerable to homicide (as is often claimed), they're highly vulnerable to suicide, so it's all the more vital that Christians approach these issues with empathy and care. But we'll see that rather than being a hateful tool of oppression, the Bible truly offers hope to those who feel alienated from their bodies.

## HOW HARRY POTTER BECAME POLITICAL

In December 2019, J. K. Rowling tweeted her support for Maya Forstater, a tax specialist who lost her job for questioning a change in British law that would not require a diagnosis of gender dysphoria to change someone's birth certificate sex. Forstater had tweeted her concern that "radically expanding the legal definition of 'women' so that it can include both males and females" made it "a meaningless concept" and would "undermine women's rights & protections for vulnerable women & girls." She added,

Some transgender people have cosmetic surgery. But most retain their birth genitals. Everyone's equality and safety should be protected, but women and girls lose out on privacy, safety and fairness if males are allowed into changing rooms, dormitories, prisons, sports teams.[1]

Forstater was fired. When she lost her appeal, Rowling responded:

Dress however you please.
Call yourself whatever you like.
Sleep with any consenting adult who'll have you.
Live your best life in peace and security.
But force women out of their jobs for stating that sex is real?
#IStandWithMaya #ThisIsNotADrill[2]

Until recently, this tweet would've been standard liberal fare. But it triggered a torrent of attacks from those who saw it as an assault on transgender identities. Rowling wasn't surprised. "I expected the threats of violence," she recalled, "to be told I was *literally killing trans people with my hate*, to be called [various misogynistic expletives]."[3] But the headlines multiplied when Daniel Radcliffe (who starred in the *Harry Potter* films) disagreed with Rowling: "Transgender women are women," he said.[4] The question is, What does it mean?

The answer might seem obvious. Radcliffe means that people who were born male, but now identify as female, should be treated as women in every respect. If transgender women are women, they should be allowed to use women's bathrooms, enter women's shelters, and compete in women's sports. Anything less, so the logic runs, is transphobic and harmful. But aside from any concerns about its implications, there is a deeper problem with the claim. If it's true that "Transgender women are women," then we no longer know what

1.   Maya Forstater (@MForstater), Twitter, September 2, 2018, 6:08 p.m., https://twitter.com/mforstater/status/1036375233723330560.
2.   J. K. Rowling (@jk_rowling), Twitter, December 19, 2019, 7:57 a.m., https://twitter.com/jk_rowling/status/1207646162813100033.
3.   J. K. Rowling, "J. K. Rowling Writes about Her Reasons for Speaking out on Sex and Gender Issues," JKRowling.com, June 10, 2020, https://www.jkrowling.com/opinions/j-k-rowling-writes-about-her-reasons-for-speaking-out-on-sex-and-gender-issues.
4.   Daniel Radcliffe, "Daniel Radcliffe Responds to J. K. Rowling's Tweets on Gender Identity," The Trevor Project, June 8, 2020, https://www.thetrevorproject.org/2020/06/08/daniel-radcliffe-responds-to-j-k-rowlings-tweets-on-gender-identity.

"woman" means. We saw in chapter 4 that the slogan "Women's rights are human rights" is worthless if there *are* no human rights. Now, the problem intensifies. If transgender women are women, there's no such thing as a woman either.

## WHAT DOES 'WOMAN' MEAN?

Until recently, "I am a woman" was a statement of biological sex. Expressions of gender (masculinity or femininity) can vary. In my culture, having long hair, wearing a skirt, and painting one's face all signal femininity. But watch the classic film *Braveheart* and you'll see long-haired, skirt-wearing, face-painting warrior men! Yet regardless of culture, "I am a woman" is a claim to biological sex. But if transgender women *are* women, this is no longer true: a biological male—who may or may not have taken hormones or undergone surgery—can be as truly a woman as I am.

A few years ago, a speaker at a Christian conference I attended used an analogy to describe male and female roles. She asked us to imagine we were building a skyscraper. Men were the architects and builders: they made the skyscraper. The women came in and decorated. The analogy seemed so utterly disconnected from anything the Bible says that I nearly left the room. But to borrow the misguided metaphor: if we take biological sex out of the definition of a woman, we swing a wrecking ball at the building itself. We have cultural paintings to hang, but no walls. For decades, feminists have been differentiating biological sex from cultural stereotypes, creating space for women to live *as* women in different ways. But if our bodies are removed from the equation, those stereotypes are all we have left.

This dismantling of the bodily reality of womanhood has led to a brewing conflict between some transgender activists and some feminists, who resent how gender stereotypes are being drawn back in. When a series of "reproductive rights" posters released by Amnesty International paired the slogan "I Stand with People in Poland" with images signaling femininity, a feminist on Twitter observed:

> Strangest thing about this is how rather than use the word 'women'
> in order to be understood they produced a load of cartoons of women

with gender stereotypical features like long flowing hair, lipstick & nail varnish. This isn't progress.[5]

"Women's Rights Are Human Rights" and "Transgender Women Are Women" turn out to be uncomfortable companions, fighting for ideological space. Responding to an article that referred to "people who menstruate," Rowling quipped: "I'm sure there used to be a word for those people. Someone help me out. Wumben? Wimpund? Woomud?"[6]

Shortly before disclosing her experience of domestic abuse, Rowling explained: "If sex isn't real, the lived reality of women globally is erased. I know and love trans people, but erasing the concept of sex removes the ability of many to meaningfully discuss their lives. It isn't hate to speak the truth."[7] But to hold classic feminist beliefs today is to be labeled a "Trans Exclusionary Radical Feminist" (or TERF) by some transgender activists. Secular feminists have lost their jobs, been canceled as speakers, and had their reputations smeared not by foes on the religious right, but by angry mobs on the progressive left.

The convention of referring to "the LGBT community" can suggest that folks identifying as LGBT+ are all aligned. But some gay and lesbian people are being called "transphobic" for expressing their preference for members of their biological sex and for voicing concern that women's rights are being compromised and that same-sex-attracted kids are being pushed to question their gender. For example, in 2019, British gay-rights activist Simon Fanshawe left the largest LGBT-rights organization in Europe (of which he was a founding member), saying that its new transgender policy risked undermining "women's sex-based rights and protections" and objecting that children in elementary school were being challenged to review their gender identity.[8] Likewise, Fred Sargeant, who organized the first gay-pride march

5.   Victoria Freeman (@v_j_freeman), Twitter, November 3, 2020, 3:31 a.m., https://twitter.com/pastasnack_e/status/1323547595839602688.

6.   J. K. Rowling (@jk_rowling), Twitter, June 6, 2020, 5:35 p.m., https://twitter.com/jk_rowling/status/1269382518362509313.

7.   J. K. Rowling (@jk_rowling), Twitter, June 6, 2020, 6:02 p.m., https://twitter.com/jk_rowling/status/1269389298664701952.

8.   Nicholas Helen, "'Anti-women' trans policy may split Stonewall," *The Times*, September 22, 2019, https://www.thetimes.co.uk/article/anti-women-trans-policy-may-split-stonewall-wfv2rp5cx.

in the United States, proclaims on his Twitter page: "Homosexuality is same-sex attraction. Biological sex is real. Sex is binary, not a spectrum."[9]

So how do transgender activists themselves speak into this? A wide range of experiences and views huddle under the transgender umbrella: from an older transgender person who thanked me for the tenderness with which I had addressed these issues after a talk I gave in England last year, to those who would have seen every word out of my mouth as hate speech. No one voice speaks for all. But it's worth hearing from individuals nonetheless.

## IT WON'T MAKE ME HAPPY, AND IT SHOULDN'T HAVE TO

In 2018, a week before elective surgery, transgender woman Andrea Long Chu wrote one of the best written *New York Times* columns I've ever read. In "My New Vagina Won't Make Me Happy. And It Shouldn't Have To," Chu declared:

> Until the day I die, my body will regard the vagina as a wound; as a result, it will require regular, painful attention to maintain. This is what I want, but there is no guarantee it will make me happier. In fact, I don't expect it to.

In mournfully evocative terms, Chu explained how little justice the definition of "gender dysphoria" (the distress some people feel at the mismatch between their biological sex and their internal sense of gender) does to the experience:

> Dysphoria feels like being unable to get warm, no matter how many layers you put on. It feels like hunger without appetite. . . . It feels like grieving. It feels like having nothing to grieve.

I'm not much of a stereotypical woman. There have been times in my life when I've felt an acute sense of failure of femininity, like it's a compulsory sport I'm terrible at playing. Despite these glimmerings

---

9.   Fred Sargeant, Twitter profile, visited November 18, 2020, https://twitter.com/FredSargeant.

of empathy, I felt my *lack* of understanding swell as I read Chu's essay. Those of us who have not experienced gender dysphoria cannot really hope to grasp it. Sometimes, we love people best by acknowledging that we don't understand.

Most transgender activists tell happy-ending stories. But Chu wrote of feeling *more* depressed and suicidal after taking hormones, of not expecting the self-inflicted wound on the horizon to usher in a new dawn of happiness, but of believing nonetheless that a transgender person's desire for surgery should not be denied. The article concludes, "There are no good outcomes in transition. There are only people, begging to be taken seriously."[10]

Struck by the bold argument and mesmerizing prose in this piece, I sought out Chu's other work. What I found continued to impress me with its authorial swagger. But the gap between Chu's viewpoint and that of any halfway traditional feminist became a chasm. The first chapter of Chu's debut book begins, "Everyone is female," and ends, "I am female. And you, dear reader, you are female, even—especially—if you are not a woman. Welcome. Sorry."[11] Chu explains: "I'll define as *female* any psychic operation in which the self is sacrificed to make room for the desires of another."[12] Here, we find less of a plea for transgender women to be taken seriously and more an artful playing with the fact that, if we have evacuated biological reality from the word "woman," we can truly say whatever we like. And here, as in the original piece, we find the primacy of choice. Not that Chu chose to experience gender dysphoria. No one would choose such a profound sense of alienation from their body. But the primacy of the right to choose one's destiny, even at the expense of one's happiness.

## NEW TRANSGENDER TREND

In one respect, Chu's experience is typical. For as long as experts have been documenting gender dysphoria, it has been observed predom-

---

10. Andrea Long Chu, "My New Vagina Won't Make Me Happy," *The New York Times*, November 22, 2018, https://www.nytimes.com/2018/11/24/opinion/sunday/vaginoplasty-transgender-medicine.html.

11. Angela Long Chu, *Females: A Concern* (Brooklyn, NY: Verso, 2019), 1–2.

12. Chu, *Females*, 11.

inantly in a small minority of biological males, who felt discomfort with their sex from childhood. For most, dysphoria resolves by adulthood. For some it does not.[13] But in the last few years, the gender imbalance has flipped. Between 2016 and 2017, the number of gender surgeries performed on females in the United States grew by 289 percent, to the point that biological *females* accounted for 70 percent of all gender surgeries.[14] In the UK, the decade from 2008 to 2018 witnessed a 4,400 percent rise in the number of teenage girls seeking gender treatments compared with the previous decade.[15] So, what is going on?

Some argue that greater social acceptance has given young girls courage to transition: the proportion of "trans boys" has not increased, but social change has allowed them to come out. Others think there's more at play. Journalist Abigail Shrier observes that many of the adolescent girls now identifying as boys, or using terms like "non-binary," "gender non-conforming," or "genderqueer," had not shown previous signs of dysphoria. She argues that much of what we are seeing is adolescent girls struggling to come to terms with their developing female bodies and often with other mental-health challenges, and seeking social acceptance by coming out as trans. In *Irreversible Damage: The Transgender Craze Seducing our Daughters*, Shrier compares "rapid onset gender dysphoria" in girls to anorexia, and suggests that the increasing numbers of young women who are seeking puberty-blocking

13.   There is much dispute about the exact numbers, but it seems that the majority of people who experience gender dysphoria in childhood find that it resolves by adulthood. See, for example J. Ristori and T. D. Steensma, "Gender Dysphoria in Childhood," *International Review of Social Psychiatry* 28, no.1 (2016):13–20.

14.   In the United States in 2016, 1,759 male-to-female surgeries were performed, versus 2,483 in 2017: a 40 percent increase. In the same year, female-to-male surgeries increased from 1,497 to 5,821: a 289 percent increase. See "2017 Plastic Surgery Statistics Report," American Society of Plastic Surgeons, https://www.plasticsurgery.org/documents/News/Statistics/2017/body-contouring-gender-confirmation-2017.pdf. See also See Madison Aitken, Thomas D. Steensma, Ray Blanchard, et al., "Evidence for an Altered Sex Ratio in Clinic-Referred Adolescents with Gender Dysphoria," *The Journal of Sexual Medicine* 12, no. 3 (March 2015): 756–63, https://doi.org/10.1111/jsm.12817.

15.   Gordon Rayner, "Minister orders inquiry into 4,000 per cent rise in children wanting to change sex," *The Telegraph*, September 16, 2018, https://www.telegraph.co.uk//politics/2018/09/16/minister-orders-inquiry-4000-per-cent-rise-children-wanting.

drugs, taking testosterone, and having their breasts removed are engaging in a form of self-harm.[16]

Shrier has no personal axe to grind. She does not have a trans-identifying child. She is Jewish, has no particular religious motivation, and she believes that for a small minority of people with severe and lasting gender dysphoria, medical intervention is warranted. But she does not think that adolescent girls should be encouraged to make life-altering, fertility-destroying choices. That's exactly what's happening. Because therapists are now in effect required to affirm an adolescent's stated trans identity, young girls who may have other mental-health struggles are being offered puberty-blocking drugs, testosterone, and ultimately mastectomies in order to enter the promised land of maleness, while their parents are told that stopping them will lead to suicide.[17]

One widely cited study asked trans-identified people, "Did any professional (such as a psychologist, counselor, religious advisor) try to make you identify only with your sex assigned at birth (in other words, try to stop you being trans)?," and found that those who said yes reported worse mental health than those who said no.[18] But the study had multiple methodological problems, including not correcting for underlying mental-health conditions, which may have caused a professional to question someone's trans identity.[19]

The incidence of suicide attempts among adolescent girls who identify as transgender is extremely high. One study found that female-to-male trans adolescents had an attempted suicide rate of 50.8 percent—the highest of any category—followed by those who identify as neither fully male nor female (41.8 percent) and then by male-

16. See Abigail Shrier, *Irreversible Damage: The Transgender Craze Seducing our Daughters* (Washington, DC: Regnery Publishing, 2020), 33, 136.

17. As Shrier points out, nearly every medical accrediting organization has endorsed "gender affirming care" as the standard for treating those who identify as transgender. Shrier, *Irreversible Damage*, 98.

18. Jack L. Turban, Noor Beckwith, Sari L. Reisner, et al., "Association between recalled exposure to gender identity conversion efforts and psychological distress and suicide attempts among transgender adults," *JAMA Psychiatry* 77, no. 1 (September 11, 2019): 68–76, https://doi.org/10.1001/jamapsychiatry.2019.2285.

19. See Roberto D'Angelo, Ema Syrulnik, Sasha Ayad, Lisa Marchiano, Dianna Theadora Kenny, and Patrick Clarke, "One Size Does Not Fit All: In Support of Psychotherapy for Gender Dysphoria," *Archives of Sexual Behavior* (2020), https://doi.org/10.1007/s10508-020-01844-2.

to-female trans adolescents (29.9 percent).[20] Those who see transgender identities as good and authentic blame this data on lack of social acceptance. This is why parents are told they must affirm their child's identity and why Rowling is accused of "literally killing trans people with [her] hate." This kind of accusation is frequently combined with the claim that trans-identifying people are murdered at a disproportionate rate. For example, Elliot (formerly Ellen) Page's public letter coming out as trans called the statistics on trans murders "staggering" and linked this murderous hate to the high rates of suicidal ideation among trans-identified people.[21] But while it is certainly possible that trans homicides have been underreported, the available evidence does *not* show that trans people are murdered at a disproportionate rate.[22]

From the other direction, those who see transgender identities as harmful will be tempted to see the levels of suicide attempts among trans-identified youth only as evidence that identifying as trans is bad for children and masks mental-health concerns, dismissing the role played by bullying and lack of empathy. These issues are so politically charged that vital research is hard to conduct, and there are no neat ideological camps. Many of the parents Shrier interviewed were secular liberals who affirmed gay marriage and transgender rights, but did not believe their daughter was trans.

Whatever our beliefs, these young people's lives matter. Mocking or dismissing those struggling with their gender identity is never the

---

20. Russell B. Toomey, Amy K. Syvertsen, Maura Shramko, "Transgender Adolescent Suicide Behavior," *Pediatrics* 142, no. 4, October 2018, https://pediatrics.aappublications.org/content/142/4/e20174218.

21. Elliot Page (@elliotpage), Instagram, December 1, 2020, https://www.instagram.com/p/CI-Q1QFBhNFg.

22. As a 2017 report expressed it, "Findings suggest that transgender people overall may not face a higher risk of being murdered than do cisgender people but that young transgender women of color almost certainly face a higher chance of being murdered." Rebecca L. Stotzer, "Data Sources Hinder Our Understanding of Transgender Murders," *American Journal of Public Health* 107, no. 9 (September 2017): 1362–63, https://www.ncbi.nlm.nih.gov/pmc/articles/PMC5551619. Most trans-identified people who are victims of homicide are black trans women, who are already more vulnerable due to their race, and 42 percent of black trans women report having taken part in income-based sex work, which also makes them more vulnerable. See Gina Martinez and Tara Law, "Two Recent Murders of Black Trans Women in Texas Reveal a Nationwide Crisis, Advocates Say," *Time*, June 5, 2019, https://time.com/5601227/two-black-trans-women-murders-in-dallas-anti-trans-violence.

right approach. But encouraging emotionally vulnerable young girls to undergo medical treatments that will distort their still-developing bodies and affect their still-developing minds is also not an act of love.

Even from a secular perspective, there are real questions about what should and should not be affirmed in people's understanding of themselves—especially if they haven't yet reached adulthood. For many, the primacy of individual freedom is a core belief. And yet most would want to stop children from killing, starving, or cutting themselves. Is a teenage girl's rejection of her female body a triumph for freedom and authenticity, or a tragic yearning born of internalized misogyny or untreated depression? Where should she look to find the truth of her gender identity: at her body, or her social media feed? If she takes puberty-blocking drugs, which Shrier notes are almost always followed by testosterone, will her resultant feelings show she was never really female, or will they disrupt a normal female body? And what about non-binary identities?

## BINARY OR NON-BINARY? BODY OR SOUL?

The British sci-fi series *Doctor Who* is one of my favorite shows. Its central character is a time-traveling alien, with two hearts, a boundless brain, and a handy ability to regenerate into a new body, when you and I would just have died. For decades, the Doctor has been regenerating as new actors have assumed the role. But the most recent incarnation has turned the Doctor into a woman. This may look like a pro-trans development. But the message seems to be that the Doctor's mind was *not* gendered and could pair equally well with a male or female body, which actually doesn't align with much transgender thinking.

While some trans people reject the "gender binary," the slogan that "Transgender women are women" reinforces the idea that one is either male or female. The claim is not that trans women are somewhere on a spectrum, but that they are women. No half-measures. Some attempt to ground this view in science, suggesting a biological reality underlying gender dysphoria: perhaps there is a "male brain" and a "female brain," and trans women have female brains. This once again raises feminist eyebrows and is highly questionable scientifically. Any slight variations between men's and women's brains represent averages, not major disconnects.[23]

Others claim that transgender women are *truly* women, not because of a biological reality that could be scientifically verified, but because psychology trumps biology. The belief is strangely spiritual. Many secular people believe in science as the final arbiter of truth and say that human beings don't have souls. But the notion of a non-physical reality that defines our gender and may or may not align with our body cuts against this stark materialism, and once again asserts the male-female binary. Once we separate our "gender identity" from anything connected to biology, it becomes impossible to pin down.

Before a recent doctor's appointment, I was asked to declare my "sex assigned at birth" and my "gender identity." Transgender advocates tend to talk as if "gender identity" is something more deeply true of the person than biological sex. For example, an educational video for Pink News describes the distress someone might feel at being "mistaken for the gender they were assigned at birth, rather than their *true* gender." This framing separates body from self and leaves us wondering, "Who assigned this *true* gender?" According to most activists, gender identity is not chosen, but discovered. It's who trans people *really* are, not something they have decided to be. But untethered from biological sex, it can also be a moving target. "Many wrongly assume that sex defines gender," explains a guide for transgender allies, "when in reality gender identity is a living, growing experience that can change over time."[24] According to this definition, transgender women may only be women temporarily, as their gender identity might change.

What precisely gender even means in this framework is unclear. The same guide offers this definition: "Gender describes our internal understanding and experience of our own gender identity."[25] But this

23. See Lise Eliot, "Neurosexism: the myth that men and women have different brains," *Nature*, February 27, 2019, https://www.nature.com/articles/d41586-019-00677-x.

24. Quoted from The Trevor Project's "Guide to Being an Ally to Transgender and Nonbinary Youth," https://www.thetrevorproject.org/wp-content/uploads/2020/03/Guide-to-Being-an-Ally-to-Transgender-and-Nonbinary-Youth.pdf.

25. Quoted from The Trevor Project's "Guide to Being an Ally to Transgender and Nonbinary Youth."

only raises the question, "What then is gender identity?" An earlier incarnation of the Doctor once had to explain time:

> People assume that time is a strict progression of cause to effect, but actually, from a non-linear, non-subjective viewpoint, it's more like a big ball of wibbly wobbly . . . timey wimey . . . stuff.

"It got away from me there," he concludes. Separated from biological sex, gender becomes just as nebulous. All we have left is stereotypes. But perhaps this is no wonder. Stripped of belief in a creator God, modern secular thinking cannot give us a coherent account of what a human being is, why we are more than a collection of cells, or how we are any different from animals. No wonder it can't tell us what it means to be male or female.

Increasing numbers of people today are leaning into the nebulousness of gender identity and using terms like "non-binary," "gender non-conforming" or "genderqueer." People vary on whether they see these identities as expressions of biological or psychological realities, or simply rejections of cultural norms. But some claim that even at a biological level, sex is not like an on-off switch, but like a dimmer light, with fully male at one end of a spectrum and fully female at the other. To argue for this perspective, they cite the reality that some people are born intersex.

## INTERSEX PEOPLE AND THE GENDER BINARY

"Intersex" describes someone born with atypical features of their sexual anatomy or sex chromosomes. Depending on which conditions are counted, estimates of the proportion of people who are born intersex vary greatly, from 1.7 percent to 0.018 percent.[26] The higher estimates include people with any kind of disorder or difference of sexual development (who may not even be aware of it), while the lower estimates restrict intersex to describe people whose sex organs are not classifiable as either male or female or whose chromosomal sex does

---

26.   See Leonard Sax, "How common is intersex? a response to Anne Fausto-Sterling," *The Journal of Sex Research* 39, no. 3 (August 2002): 174–78, https://doi.org/10.1080/00224490209552139.

not match their anatomy. For example, a few years back, a friend of mine gave birth to a baby whose body looked predominantly female, but who turned out to be chromosomally male. But whether the term should apply to one person in 60 or one person in 6,000, some people are undoubtedly born with significant intersex conditions. Is this the key to unlock the shackles that have bound us to the gender binary?

First, it's important for Christians to recognize that intersex people are precious human beings made in the image of God—not pawns in a political fight—and that many of us are undereducated about intersex conditions and distinguishing them from transgender identities. Christian parents of intersex children often feel isolated as they face the unique challenges of raising their kids, and perhaps having to explain to them at an early age that they will be unable have biological children.

Second, however, to say that babies born intersex disprove the reality of the male-female binary misses the fact that it was only *because* of the male-female binary that these babies exist at all. In September 2019, a pregnant woman posted a series of photos parodying gender reveals. In one photo, she held balloons spelling, "Gender is a construct." But while much of what we associate with gender is culturally determined, biological sex is not. According to a previous Facebook post, this woman's pregnancy was made possible by a sperm donation rather than a sexual relationship. But the reality remains that the baby in her womb exists because of the sexual binary, and that if her child one day has biological children, it will only be because of that binary. Today, people often present the sex binary as *oppressive*. But at its very heart, the male-female binary is *creative*. Rather than cutting against diversity, God created us so that deep intimacy across this diversity would generate new life.

So, where does this leave people with intersex conditions? What does the Bible say to my friend's child? And what does it say to the trans woman who approached me after my talk at a Christian conference, or to Andrea Long Chu, who was raised Presbyterian, or to the adolescent girls taking testosterone? Does the Bible speak to today's complex situations?

## JESUS'S HARD TEACHING

As we have seen, the Bible's first words about sex and gender are that God created humans—male and female—in his image (Gen. 1:26–27). When the Pharisees ask Jesus, "Is it lawful to divorce one's wife for any cause?," he responds:

> Have you not read that he who created them from the beginning made them male and female, and said, 'Therefore a man shall leave his father and his mother and hold fast to his wife, and the two shall become one flesh'? So they are no longer two but one flesh. What therefore God has joined together, let not man separate." (Matt. 19:4–6)

Jesus affirms both the binary of male and female in creation *and* the binding of male *to* female in marriage. The Pharisees try to trap him by asking why Moses allowed divorce. Jesus replies, "Because of your hardness of heart" and adds, "I say to you: whoever divorces his wife except for sexual immorality, and marries another woman, commits adultery" (Matt. 19:8–9). Jesus is sometimes misrepresented as not caring about sexual ethics. But here, as in the Sermon on the Mount, Jesus doesn't loosen the Old Testament law on sexual faithfulness. He tightens it.

In Jesus's context, as in ours, this strong repudiation of divorce is countercultural. His disciples respond, "If such is the case of a man with his wife, it is better not to marry." Jesus replies:

> Not everyone can receive this saying, but only those to whom it is given. For there are eunuchs who have been so from birth, and there are eunuchs who have been made eunuchs by men, and there are eunuchs who have made themselves eunuchs for the sake of the kingdom of heaven. Let the one who is able to receive this receive it. (Matt. 19:11–12)

While increasing numbers of people in our culture identify as transgender, you'd struggle to find a 21st-century Westerner identifying as a eunuch. So, what is Jesus saying?

As we saw in chapter 1, eunuchs were males who had been castrated to perform a particular cultural function. While still identified as male, they were cut out of the possibility of fatherhood and likely denied marriage. Jesus's allusion to "eunuchs who have been made eunuchs by men" refers to this. Mosaic law stopped eunuchs from entering God's temple, but eunuchs were fully embraced by the church. In fact, one of the first conversion stories we read in Acts is of a eunuch (Acts 8:26–40). But Jesus also describes two other groups: those who were eunuchs "from birth" and those who have "made themselves eunuchs for the sake of the kingdom of heaven." What does he mean?

First, we must notice that while Jesus affirmed the sex binary in creation, he also recognizes that some people *from birth* are not equipped with standard-issue sex organs. Like castrated eunuchs, these people would likely not have been eligible for marriage and would have experienced various forms of social exclusion. But they were fully welcomed among God's people. Jesus's words offer vital truth for Christians with intersex conditions. Our value as Christians is not tied to our reproductive ability. It's tied to Christ.

Second, while Jesus's answer to the Pharisees strongly supports marriage, his response to his disciples affirms those who have "made themselves eunuchs"—sacrificed marriage and parenthood—"for the sake of the kingdom of heaven." For Jewish men of Jesus's day, building a family was a top priority. But while Jesus has such a high view of marriage that his disciples were shocked, he also ranks God's kingdom before marriage and family (e.g., Matt. 19:29). Some believers then as now serve God best as single people. Paul was one striking example of fruitful singleness. But how do we know Jesus wasn't referring to people castrating themselves for the sake of the kingdom of heaven, as some transgender advocates suggest?[27]

Voluntary castration was a known religious practice in Jesus's day, but it was associated with pagan cults. Tom Holland describes a cult in first-century Galatia like this:

> The *Galli*, men dressed as woman, were servants of Cybele, the Mother Goddess who sat enthroned amid the highest peaks of Galatia; and the mark of their submission to this most powerful and venerable

27.  See, for example, Austen Hartke, *Transforming: The Bible and the Lives of Transgender People* (Westminster John Knox: Louisville, 2018), 106–8.

of the region's gods was the severing with a knife or sharp stone of their testicles.[28]

Writing to Christians in Galatia, Paul argues powerfully against those who said Gentile believers should be circumcised and quips, "I wish those who unsettle you would emasculate themselves!" (Gal. 5:12). This may be a critical reference to the Galli. As Paul was rejecting even circumcision of Gentiles as a demonstration of devotion to Christ, the idea that Jesus was talking about castration as a way of expressing devotion to the kingdom of heaven is unthinkable. But what about the most famous line in Paul's letter to the Galatians, in which the boundaries of male and female are broken down?

## NO MALE AND FEMALE, ALL ONE IN CHRIST

Circumcision marked Jewish males as heirs of God's promises to Abraham. But in Galatians, Paul argues that Jesus alone is "Abraham's seed." This is the context for these glorious, lifegiving lines:

> There is neither Jew nor Greek, there is neither slave nor free, there is no male and female, for you are all one in Christ Jesus. And if you are Christ's, then you are Abraham's offspring, heirs according to promise. (Gal. 3:28–29)

Gentiles don't need circumcision to realize God's promises. Slaves, who would not inherit in the ancient world, become "sons of God." Women are as much Abraham's heirs as Jewish men are. Marriage (which some commentators think Paul means by "male and female") is not required. Anyone—regardless of ethnic background, religious heritage, social status, biological sex, or marriage status—can be in Christ. Jesus has them covered.

So, are male and female simply erased in Christ? No. Paul clearly affirms the spiritual equality of men and women in Galatians 3:28. But in multiple other passages he distinguishes between male and female roles (Eph. 5:22–33). Using Galatians 2:28 to justify the erasure of male

28. Holland, *Dominion*, 83.

and female would be like using it to justify promiscuous sex between believers on the grounds that we are all *one body* in Christ. We need to understand Paul's words in the context of the whole letter, and of the whole New Testament.

## NO MARRIAGE IN HEAVEN

Another text to which people sometimes appeal to argue that the Bible erases male and female is Jesus's conversation with the Sadducees, who did not believe in the future resurrection. The Sadducees described a woman being widowed by seven brothers and asked Jesus whose wife she would be at the resurrection. Jesus replied:

> You are wrong, because you know neither the Scriptures nor the power of God. For in the resurrection they neither marry nor are given in marriage, but are like angels in heaven. (Matt. 22:29–30)

Some argue that this means we will no longer be male and female in the new creation, so transgender identities are valid now. But the point Jesus is making is not about biological sex, it's about marriage. As we saw in chapter 2, marriage points to a greater reality. When the wedding of the Lamb comes, we will no longer need human marriage. The absence of sexual relationships in the New Creation will change one aspect of how many of us exist as male and female humans. But this does not mean male and female are erased. The angels we meet in the Bible are represented as male.[29] And the one person we see progress through death to resurrection life (rather than just being brought back from death) is Jesus, who remained male. God made us male and female from the beginning. The promised resurrection of our male and female bodies is the ultimate proof that they are truly good and that they embody our true selves.

---

29.   For example, the angel Gabriel, who tells Mary she's going to have a baby.

## GOODNESS OF THE BODY

When Christianity was born in the first century, one of its distinctives was belief in the goodness of the body. Many contemporary belief systems promised an escape from the flesh. For example, the Greek philosopher Plato taught that the highest reward for a man's soul was to be promoted into disembodied bliss, while souls that lacked virtue could be reincarnated as women, and potentially move down the chain of animals from there. Within this framework, the soul was better off without the body, and men's bodies were better than women's.

This isn't what the Bible teaches.

In the Bible, both men and women enter the kingdom of God *as* men and women, because they are in Christ. Both men and women are made in the image of God. Rather than seeing our bodies as prisons to escape, the Bible asserts that the ultimate spiritual being *became* flesh in the person of Jesus: not just for a time, but forever. The promise of Christianity is not the promise of an everlasting, incorporeal soul. It's the promise of a resurrected body.[30]

This integrated view of humanness that anchors the true self to the body cuts against transgender ideology, which separates our "sex assigned at birth" from our true "gender identity." And it offers an alternative to the pseudo-resurrection experience promised by transition. For trans-identifying people today, taking hormones and submitting to surgeries to conform their bodies to the supposedly deeper reality of their gender identity is seen not as assault, but as healing: bringing body and self into harmony. Transitioning (whether social or surgical) is a kind of resurrection. Calling someone by their pre-transition name is known as "deadnaming."

So, what alternative hope does Christianity offer to those who feel alienated from their bodies, like their true selves are not seen, like there is something deep within them that is out of joint with their flesh?

---

30.  Even when Jesus warned his followers not to fear "those who kill the body but cannot kill the soul," he reinforced the idea that soul and body belong together after death: "Rather fear him who can destroy both soul and body in hell" (Matt. 10:28).

# PAINFUL, RESURRECTION HOPE

With my first two babies, the epidural worked. I spent hours in early labor groaning as each contraction hit. But then I got to the hospital and, thanks to a kindly needle, the pain stopped. My body continued to do its work. I rested until it was time to push. With my third child, the epidural failed. As I entered the phase known as transition, my body started to do the strange things women's bodies do in childbirth—shaking, trembling. I dreaded contractions as they came like rapid fire. But when my son was born, my pain—at last—was worth it. Paul uses this exact experience to help the Roman Christians understand their suffering:

> For we know that the whole creation has been groaning together in the pains of childbirth until now. And not only the creation, but we ourselves, who have the firstfruits of the Spirit, groan inwardly as we wait eagerly for adoption as sons, the redemption of our bodies. (Rom. 8:22–23)

The Bible tells a story in which our bodies, male or female, are created very good. But sin has cut us off from God and alienated us from his world, from each other, and from our very flesh. Even those of us born with healthy bodies will find they let us down, bring us suffering, and finally expire. For those trusting in Christ, the redemption of our bodies is coming. To be a Christian now is to groan inwardly and to wait eagerly, like a laboring mother. But when that day comes, whatever pain or loss or disappointment we feel now will be undone. However alienated we feel from our flesh, it will be redeemed. And we know this because of the painful, agonizing work of the greatest man who ever died.

You see, at the heart of Christianity is the horrific death and stunning resurrection of the one true image of the invisible God (Col. 1:15). Jesus was the perfect man. But he was no gender stereotype. He had the power to silence storms, command angels, and kill death. But his arms held babies, his hands healed the sick, and his words brought comfort to the weary, rejected, and weak. When his friend Lazarus died, Jesus wept. Like a mother hen gathering her chicks under her wings, Jesus longed to gather the children of Jerusalem to himself (Matt. 23:37). To see God's kingdom, Jesus says, is to be born again (John 3:3).

No follower of Jesus need hold to rigid gender stereotypes, in which men make skyscrapers and women decorate their walls. Instead, we must cling to our Savior. He is the one who knows us to our core and loves us to death and beyond. He made our bodies, and he holds our hearts. Our deepest identity lies in him. "For you have died, and your life is hidden with Christ in God," Paul writes. "When Christ who is your life appears, then you also will appear with him in glory" (Col. 3:3–4).

For those who feel alienated from their sex, who feel like they can't get warm in their bodies, no matter how many layers they put on, Jesus offers hope. Not the hope of a differently sexed body, but the hope of a new reality that no longer feels like labor pains. The transgender person I met after my talk in England thanked me for treating these questions with tenderness. But Jesus's tenderness utterly surpasses ours. It's the tenderness of the God who likens his love to that of a nursing mother (Isa. 49:15). We can trust our fragile bodies to this God, however out of joint with them we feel, because he loves us with an everlasting love. One day he will wipe away every tear from our eyes and make our groaning bodies new.

When Mulan returned to her hometown, the father whose place she took in battle said, "One warrior knows another. You were always there. Yet I see you for the first time." But when we see Jesus, we'll return to the one who formed us in our mother's womb, and who took our place when he died on the cross. He's seen us every day we've lived and knows us better than we know ourselves. However hopeless life feels now, he's written the script for our eternity. And if we simply put our trust in him, our story's end will be unfathomably good.

# CALL TO
# LOVING ARMS

"Can't you hear it?"

I didn't need a car in London. But when we moved to America, my husband taught me to drive on the manual-shift car he'd bought second-hand at age 16. I struggled to learn when to change gears. I'd start in first and accelerate until the car was pleading for second. Focused on the road ahead, I'd miss the tell-tale sound. "Can't you hear it?" Bryan would ask. I'd rush to switch from accelerator to clutch, grab the gear stick, pull it back, and slide it across so I could push it forward again into second. And so we'd go on, until the car was crying out for third.

Perhaps, like me, you're a follower of Jesus, and you want to keep your foot on the gas. There is so much that we Christians need to do, and so far we need to go to see people from every tribe and nation won for Christ. But after 12 years living in America, I'm convinced that in order to make progress we must change gears. Rather than just ramming our foot down, we must pull the gear stick back and do the hard work of repentance before shifting into second or third.

In particular, white Christians like me must recognize the ways in which our tribe has been complicit in the pain of black Americans: from slavery to segregation to racial inequality today. Acknowledging this sin can feel like a step back. Some see it as a distraction from the vital work of sharing the gospel. But what if the failure truly to listen to the voices of black brothers and sisters and to reckon with this history of sin is holding our evangelism back, just as my failure to listen to my car kept me from changing into second gear?

We might worry that proclaiming "black lives matter" affirms a broader progressive agenda that also celebrates LGBT+ identities. But what if our failure to fight for racial equality while also upholding biblical sexual ethics allows that progressive wedding of ideas to stand unquestioned? If we don't fight for the biblical goals of racial justice and equality, we're playing into the script that says Christian sexual ethics come bundled with oppression. In order to make progress, it's vital that we unyoke these ideas. To show where progressives are wrong, we must also freely acknowledge where they are right.

Whatever our racial background, we Christians must also repent of the ways we've allowed *actual* homophobia—fear, hatred, and mistrust of gay and lesbian people—to infect our churches. Too often, LGBT+ people outside the church have only heard a message of hate. Too often, we've left our same-sex-attracted siblings within the church shivering in the dark, believing they're unwanted and unloved. If you want to pour lighter fuel on sexual temptation, you leave someone alone. But if we want same-sex-attracted Christians to thrive, we must embrace them with loving arms. This doesn't mean affirming same-sex romance. It means obeying the Bible, which calls us to bear each other's burdens (Gal. 6:2) and to love each other deeply (1 Pet. 4:8). What's more, in a world in which people block their ears to the gospel because they think we're homophobic bigots, the faithful, same-sex-attracted Christians in our congregations are a God-given SWAT team to burst through those defenses. There is no more powerful way to testify to Jesus in this generation than to turn away from sexual and romantic fulfilment because you believe in a better love.

We must also acknowledge the ways in which we've failed to follow Jesus in his treatment of women. Rather than sidelining women, we must celebrate women's gospel ministry, cultivate women's theological growth, and encourage women as they serve the Lord, whether in the home or in the workplace. In a world where women are pushed into commitment-free sex, the counterculture of the church should affirm both marriage and singleness as compelling options for Christians, rather than making women who aren't married or don't have children feel marginalized. And against the history of shaming women for having babies outside of marriage, our churches should validate women who have chosen to keep their baby against all social pressure to abort, and offer the extended family and practical support that single mothers need.

In a world where transitioning to the opposite sex or rejecting the gender binary has come to seem for some like salvation, we must affirm the goodness of male and female bodies without clinging to unbiblical gender stereotypes. If Jesus cooked for his disciples, wept with his friends, and took babies in his arms, we don't need to pretend that manhood is just about loving cars, watching sports, and lifting weights. And if Jesus had some of his most important theological conversations with women, we must not act as if women only care about cooking and clothes. Christians must repent of the ways in which our embrace of cultural stereotypes has made some people feel as if they don't belong in their own skin. We must take those who experience gender dysphoria seriously and sit with them in their discomfort, not claiming to understand when we don't, and not affirming a gender identity that goes against their sex, but listening to each person's story and seeking to support them however we can. This action may not always be received as love. God's rule over our lives is heresy to modern, self-determining ears. But we must speak the truth with tenderness and not let our sin take the wheel.

On all these fronts, we must fight hard with the weapon God has given us: self-sacrificing, unrelenting love. Rather than shouting progressives who seek love and justice down, let's call them in with a Jesus song: his song of good news for the historically oppressed, his song of love across racial and ethnic difference, his song that summons men and women, married and single, young and old, weak and strong, joyful and hurting, rich and destitute, into eternal love with him. Let's fight with love and sing the song with which we'll one day overcome.

Can you hear it?

# ACKNOWLEDGEMENTS

This book happened quickly, and so will the thank yous.

I'm thankful to Collin Hansen, Matt Smethurst, and Ivan Mesa at The Gospel Coalition for being willing to jump and for making all things needful happen in record time. I'm thankful to Rachel Gilson for telling me to write this book, and for being my first reader, best counselor, and daily source of encouragement. I'm grateful for Claude Atcho and Steven Harris, who gave me expert feedback; and for Sam Allberry, who read the whole book the night I sent it to him: the sign of a great friend! I feel greatly blessed by the support of Christine Caine, who prayed for me and spurred me on, despite having so many other demands on her time. These brothers and sisters in Christ are a gift. God knows I work best with a team.

I'm thankful to all the people who let me use their stories in this book, and to my family, who endured my writing frenzy once again. I could not write in public on such controversial themes if I didn't know, in private, I am loved. Finally, I'm thankful to the One person who thinks I am worth dying for, and who will hold me through eternity. He is my resurrection and my life.

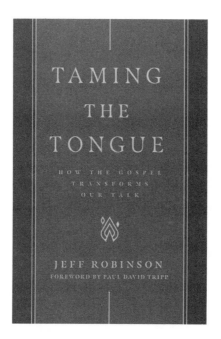

TAMING

THE

TONGUE

HOW THE GOSPEL
TRANSFORMS
OUR TALK

JEFF ROBINSON
FOREWORD BY PAUL DAVID TRIPP

"This book hit home with me, perhaps because some of my greatest regrets have come from ways I've misused words—confidences I didn't keep, criticism I was too eager to offer, bragging to make myself seem important, dominating the conversation when I should have listened. I've also misused words by keeping silent when I should have come clean, when I should have offered praise, when I should have spoken up. These and many more insights on how we use our words are covered in this brief but wisdom-filled book—a great book to read prayerfully on your own, but even better to use to discuss with a small group."

NANCY GUTHRIE, author and Bible teacher

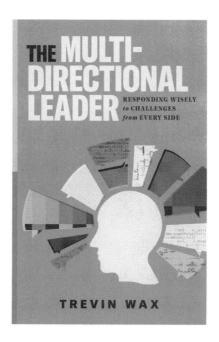

"Trevin Wax writes with keenness of insight, pastoral wisdom, and prophetic forcefulness. In this book he articulates the pressure today's Christian leaders feel from every direction. Wax remains one of my most reliable counselors for leading in a rapidly shifting context."

J. D. GREEAR, pastor, The Summit Church, Raleigh-Durham, North Carolina; president, Southern Baptist Convention

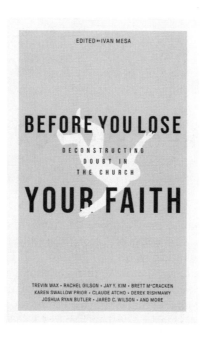

EDITED BY IVAN MESA

# BEFORE YOU LOSE

DECONSTRUCTING
DOUBT IN
THE CHURCH

# YOUR FAITH

TREVIN WAX · RACHEL GILSON · JAY Y. KIM · BRETT M<sup>c</sup>CRACKEN
KAREN SWALLOW PRIOR · CLAUDE ATCHO · DEREK RISHMAWY
JOSHUA RYAN BUTLER · JARED C. WILSON · AND MORE

"Over the years I've met many younger Christians who aren't sure they can or even should bother any longer with this ancient faith. Some end up leaving the church with a sense of liberation. Others feel as though they're falling with no one to catch them. The church ought to be the place where they feel safe asking hard questions and sharing honest doubts. The distinguished contributors to *Before You Lose Your Faith* write with sympathy and understanding. They can help anxious readers reconstruct a stronger, lasting faith in our trustworthy Savior."

COLLIN HANSEN, vice president of content and editor in chief of The Gospel Coalition and host of the Gospelbound podcast

# TGC THE GOSPEL COALITION

The Gospel Coalition (TGC) supports the church in making disciples of all nations, by providing gospel-centered resources that are trusted and timely, winsome and wise.

Guided by a Council of more than 40 pastors in the Reformed tradition, TGC seeks to advance gospel-centered ministry for the next generation by producing content (including articles, podcasts, videos, courses, and books) and convening leaders (including conferences, virtual events, training, and regional chapters).

In all of this we want to help Christians around the world better grasp the gospel of Jesus Christ and apply it to all of life in the 21st century. We want to offer biblical truth in an era of great confusion. We want to offer gospel-centered hope for the searching.

Join us by visiting TGC.org so you can be equipped to love God with all your heart, soul, mind, and strength, and to love your neighbor as yourself.